VINTAGE JEWELLERY

SOURCEBOOK

Designers, styles and stockists for
costume and fine jewellery

Caroline Cox

CARLTON
BOOKS

To Joanna and Clive

Design copyright © Carlton Books Limited 2010
Text © Caroline Cox 2010

First published as *Vintage Jewellery* in 2010.
This abridged edition published in 2013
by Carlton Books Limited
20 Mortimer Street
London W1T 3JW

10 9 8 7 6 5 4 3 2 1

ISBN 978 1 78097 428 6
Printed and bound in China

Senior Executive Editor: Lisa Dyer
Managing Art Director: Lucy Coley
Designer: A&E Design
Copy Editor: Jane Donovan
Picture Researcher: Jenny Meredith
Production Manager: Maria Petalidou

PREVIOUS PAGE Gold and
Swarovski crystal cuff
bracelet, circa 1950s.

RIGHT A necklace from Alan
Andersen uses vintage
stones in a new design.

MIX
Paper
FSC FSC® C101537

Contents

'00s–'10s   'I0s   '20s   '30s   '40s

Introduction

Whether it's the fire and ice of a Harry Winston diamond, the milky glow of an Akoya cultured pearl, the warmth of a Victorian rose-gold ring or the chill of an Art Deco platinum parure, the desire to decorate the body with fabulous jewels has always been a natural human preoccupation. Body ornament excites our imagination and, when mixed with the mysterious alchemy of gems and jewellery, magic is made. The beauty of precious gemstones has been lauded since the beginning of civilization.

Jewellery may once have been our oldest form of currency but it is much more than a symbol of wealth and social status. From the pagan belief that a string around the neck kept the soul from flying away from the body to the ostentatious flaunting of jewellery won from a succession of rich paramours by the grand horizontales of the *belle époque*, jewellery has always been a potent expression of the zeitgeist. Marilyn Monroe's paen to the rock, "Diamonds are a Girl's Best Friend", fused our cultural obsession with the jewel on film in *Gentlemen Prefer Blondes* (1953), while Grace Kelly's elegant string

of pearls was a symbol of her cool patrician beauty. The ups and downs of the love affair between Elizabeth Taylor and Richard Burton were made manifest in the huge gems he gave her, including the celebrated La Peregrina pearl. More recently, the couple's modern-day counterparts, Brad Pitt and Angelina Jolie, did things differently – in 2009 they collaborated with Asprey of London on the Protector, a range designed to benefit the Education Partnership for Children in Conflict.

We have a lexicon of jewellery forms to dip into; rings, for instance, have evolved from being symbols of ownership to a dazzling expression of status, from the industrial-sized gems worn by the ace-faces of hip-hop in the 1990s through to the work of innovative designers such as Catherine Provost and Marie-Hélène de Taillac, both renowned for using gems in very contemporary ways. The brooch, the only piece of jewellery that necessitates the wearing of clothes, is perhaps the most idiosyncratic in its subject matter. Queen Victoria loved brooches and had a set of three in the shape of bows

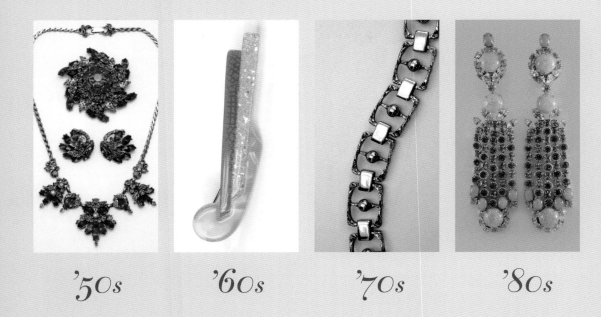

'50s   '60s   '70s   '80s

made by Garrard, which are still occasionally worn today by Queen Elizabeth II; in 1949, maverick artist Salvador Dalí designed a pair of ruby-encrusted lips with pearl teeth looking as if set to jump from a lapel to give a vicious nip. Earrings are playful – at their lengthiest, it seems, when hair fashions are short and leave a lobe as an optimum site for display. With the chic flapper bobs of the 1920s, triangles and trapezoid earrings reflected the dynamism of metropolitan life, making women seem like beautiful machines; in the 1980s a logo mania took hold and a huge double "C"-emblazoned Chanel clip in faux gold gave instant cachet.

In the twenty-first century jewellery has never been more inventive and one of the most exciting areas of development is in *haute joaillerie* produced by fashion's most prestigious houses. Labels such as Versace, Gucci and Dior challenge the role of companies such as Cartier and Bulgari, which have dominated the luxury market for generations. Avant-garde designers such as Shaun Leane for McQueen parlay their catwalk experiments into ranges of wearable and desirable jewellery that are clearly the collectables of the future, and if you need a quick fix from the privacy of your own home, Butler & Wilson – who have produced some of the sparkliest of costume jewellery since the 1970s – can now be purchased with a click of a remote from shopping TV.

This book charts almost 100 years of jewellery history and will help you to identify each significant style and designer, and to know in which direction your collecting passion lies. Enjoy!

FROM LEFT TO RIGHT Silver and pearl Kalo pendant; celluloid hair comb, circa 1910; Venetian beads; Hobé rhinestone pendant brooch; Victorian Revival brass and rhinestone hand pin by Coro; Victorian Revival parure; musical note pin by Lea Stein; pewter bracelet by Gilles Vidal; clip chandelier opal earrings with Swarovski crystals by Robert Sorrell.

1890–1910:
Divinely Decadent

Cartier, Fabergé, Tiffany & Co., Boucheron… fabulous names that conjure up the glitter of diamonds, the sheen of pearls and the glint of emeralds and rubies – and names that could never have achieved their evocative power in the early twentieth century before the rise of the industrialists, middle-class metropolitans with bottomless pockets of "new money".

The notion that a jewellery house could have its own signature piece or that a designer could craft an object of beauty to commission is an invention of the modern world. Traditionally the most fabulous pieces belonged to aristocratic dynasties who passed the "family jewels" down from generation to generation, having the stones re-set or cut according to changes in taste and fashion. With the rise of a new *haute-bourgeoisie* who had money to burn and a taste for the trappings of status, jewellery became desirous not just for the stones in the settings but also for the magical maker's name.

During this period the most prestigious firms consolidated their reputations both at home and abroad, becoming mighty brands that continue to dominate the market today. In the same era came others whose approach was revolutionary: René Lalique, Philippe Wolfers and Josef Hoffmann, innovative artist-jewellers who were also to gain a global following, albeit on a smaller scale.

Such jewellery was worn against limpid silks, soft crepe de Chine and pintucked lace, giving Edwardian fashion a sensuality that had barely existed before. A woman's body may have been rigidly encased in heavy corsetry to gain the required S-bend silhouette or "pouter-pigeon" look, but it was also swathed in a variety of flirtatiously beribboned garments. The look was one of a lascivious gift, ready to be unwrapped by a besotted beau, who had been bewitched by the sound of *froufrou*, the name given to the rustling sound of taffeta petticoats brushing against the underside of a heavy outer skirt. Cream, grey and lavender were perfectly accented by white on white jewellery, making diamonds set in platinum mounts popular. Queen Alexandra introduced one of the key looks of this period when she wore several rows of pearls set into a *collier de chien*, or dog collar, stunning when displayed against her pale swan-like neck. Fashion became more fluid during this decade, anticipating the more liberated styles of the 1920s, clearly reflected in the switchback curves of Art Nouveau design.

OPPOSITE Queen Alexandra set the vogue for the pearl and diamond *collier de chien* in the Edwardian period. She sports a style that accentuates her swan-like neck in 1889.

▶ Semiprecious stones

Semiprecious stones are favoured in Art Nouveau jewellery over the ostentatious glitter of diamonds, rubies and emeralds. The softer colour schemes of the new aesthetic required stones such as opal, moonstone and river pearl for their effects. This enamelled silver pendant with semiprecious stones is by Ernestine Mills.

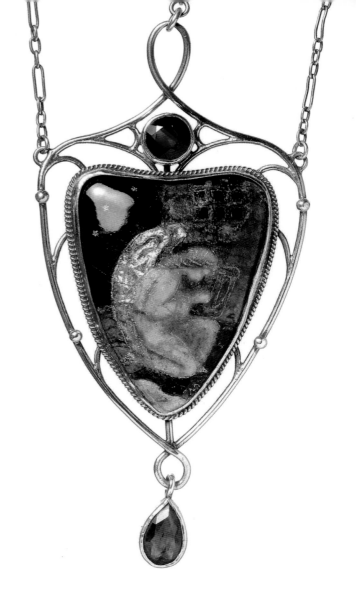

▲ Enamel

Art Nouveau is recognizable by the use of enamel work on metals, such as pewter or silver, rather than gold or platinum. In this enamel and pressed steel marcasite brooch the ornamentation comes from shades of navy, light blue and yellow enamel rather than an emphasis on the effects of light on sparkling gemstones.

Key looks
of the decades
1890–1910

Bijouterie

Highly decorated designs incorporating the use of smaller gemstones with a variety of other techniques, all worked in an integrated piece, took prominence over large showy gemstones in settings.

Celtic knots

The Celtic knot was both a fashionable and desirable decorative format during the later Arts and Crafts and Art Nouveau periods, promoted by such jewellery designers as Archibald Knox and Liberty of London.

◀ Opals and moonstones

The moonstone was used by many designers in this period including Danish jeweller Georg Jensen, as seen in this silver brooch. Moonstone is a translucent gemstone with a blue-white sheen and is said to bring good luck to the wearer. The misty dream-like effects it produced suited the spirit of Art Nouveau.

▼ Themes from nature

Nature was the main source of inspiration in Art Nouveau jewellery as its adherents tried to break the shackles of Victorian design that looked backwards rather than forwards. Eschewing any sort of revivalism, designers used flora and fauna for their motifs, as clearly seen in this selection of brooches from 1901.

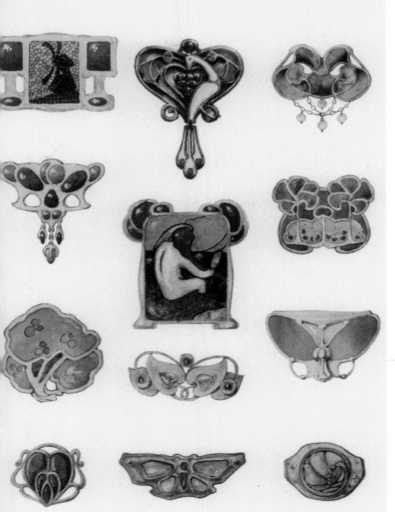

▲ The femme fatale

Art Nouveau jewellery featured the *femme fatale*, a mysterious woman whose erotic appearance was beautiful but potentially deadly. This Belle du Nuit brooch, circa 1900, depicts a bat-like female figure carved from ivory with *plique-à-jour* enamel wings scattered with diamond collets set against a crescent moon.

L'Art Nouveau

The whiplash curling lines and elaborate arabesques of Art Nouveau ran rampant over jewellery design in the period known as the *belle époque* (1890–1910). Art Nouveau, or "new art", was seductive and sinuous, derived from an essentially exoticized nature with recurring motifs such as dragonflies, peacocks and death's-head moths combined with the hallucinatory experimentation of French symbolism, the heady seduction of the work of artist Aubrey Beardsley and the *femme fatales* of Czech artist Alphonse Mucha. It was the first truly international design movement of the twentieth century, and is called, variously, *Jugendstil* in Germany, *Sezessionstil* in Vienna, *Arte Joven* ("Young Style") in Spain and, owing to its close association with the work of Louis Comfort Tiffany, the Tiffany Style in America. The curvilinear aesthetic of Art Nouveau was equally at home in the large-scale architectural projects of Antoni Gaudí in Barcelona or Victor Horta in Brussels and in the more intimate jewellery designs of René Lalique in Paris and Philippe Wolfers in Brussels.

What marked Art Nouveau jewellery out was the way it broke away from the revivalist styles of the nineteenth century and what was considered "the tyranny of the diamond". Artists began to concentrate on nature, above all else, as a source of inspiration. The discovery of Japanese art in the mid-nineteenth century opened many a designer's eyes to the beauty of asymmetry, simplicity of composition and economy of line; when combined with the decadent mysteries of Baudelaire's symbolism, a new aesthetic was born.

Many Art Nouveau pieces incorporated organic forms *à la Japonisme* combined with the use of small stones studded over the whole rather than the more showy single gems of the Victorian period. Baroque or river pearls were much sought after for their irregular shape and opals were favoured because of their milky bloom, so different from the ice-cold glint of diamonds. New combinations of metals and semiprecious stones were used to emphasize colour with enamel providing lustrous hues and pastel shading. This vitreous material, a mix of powdered silica, potash and metallic oxide colourants, was a feature of traditional Japanese art, in particular the *inro*, a compartmented box for personal effects. The discovery by Art Nouveau designers led to its use in the metal surfaces of jewellery employing a variety of revivalist techniques such as:

* *Basse-taille*, in which glass enamel is applied to a metal surface that has been engraved deeply enough to hold the enamel when heated, and with sides high enough to keep each colour separate.

* *Champlevé*, where the metal background is etched or carved and then filled with enamel and polished to produce a flat surface.

* *Cloisonné*, where the sections of enamel are defined by wire, as in a stained glass window.

The subjects of this new type of jewellery were organic in the extreme, such as vines, water lilies, irises and anemone, all chosen for their ability to be rendered as the most sinuous of tendrils, full of rhythmic energy. The animal kingdom was similarly depicted in all its emotionally charged complexities to reflect the duality of nature. Fauna could be serene and life-affirming, such as swans, swallows and peacocks, or fraught with danger ,such as serpents, bats, mythological fire-breathing dragons, sinister vultures and wasps.

ABOVE In this 1899 poster, "La Plume", by Alphonse Mucha, the enigmatic Art Nouveau femme fatale is depicted as an elemental force of nature, whose swirling tresses find echo in the whiplash lines of early twentieth-century jewellery design.

Philippe Wolfers

Brussels was the most Art Nouveau of cities with a prodigious output of the style in all its forms. Architects Victor Horta and Henri van der Velde found enthusiastic patrons for the most avant-garde of projects, including the Tassel House, and the country's booming industrial economy meant money was readily available for *bijoux de luxe*.

Son of master-goldsmith Louis Wolfers, Philippe (1858–1929) entered his father's workshop as an apprentice in 1875, where he received extensive training in jewellery-making techniques. In the 1880s he began crafting a series of ewers in gold and silver decorated with asymmetrical floral motifs that anticipated the Art Nouveau style and influenced the jewellery he began producing from 1890 in his own workshop, culminating in a successful collection exhibited at the Paris Salon in 1900.

Much of the jewellery created by Philippe Wolfers transforms the languid lines of Art Nouveau into theatrically decadent excess. He had a particular penchant for the *femme fatale*, a key motif in Symbolism, that retained its popularity in Art Nouveau design. The *femme fatale* was a woman of such dazzling beauty that she became a harbinger of death to any man enraptured by her mesmerizing, yet ultimately fatal beauty – a stereotype of femininity, stretching back to Eve and her forbidden fruit in the Garden of Eden. The fatal woman gained currency in the new century as men looked on with alarm at the vociferous movement for women's suffrage and the fight for the right to vote. This was a very different woman to the one who had dominated most of the nineteenth century as a domesticated keeper of hearth and home; as women discovered themselves socially, politically, and above all sexually (as documented in the work of the father of psychoanalysis, Sigmund Freud, based in Vienna), so men retreated, their minds beset by ancient fears. The *femme fatale*

was back, mysterious and seductively dangerous – a woman who could lure men to their doom.

The *femme fatale* is used in many of Wolfers' jewellery designs such as his Medusa pendant, on which she is depicted surrounded by a menagerie of her peculiars that take the uncanny forms of bats, insects and serpents. Brooches shape-shift into pearl-studded dragonflies; diamond- and ruby-encrusted orchids act as exotic hair ornaments fashioned from enamel and gold. Notably, Wolfers was one of the first modern designers to use ivory, in plentiful supply due to Belgium's presence in the Congo. His work is marked by incredible technical virtuosity, especially in the use of *plique-à-jour* enamelling, considered the most difficult of enamelling techniques. Thin veins of silver or gold filigree wire are fused into a vitreous enamel with the backing metal removed after firing. The resulting translucent effect is designed to evoke the effect of light glimpsed through a stained glass window – hence the name *plique-à-jour*, or "glimpse of day".

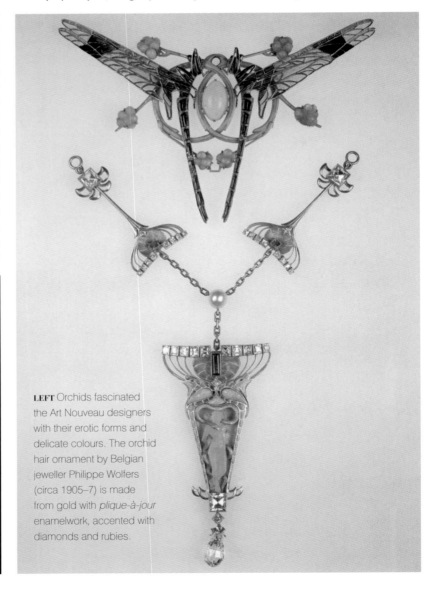

BELOW Art Nouveau designers introduced new aesthetics into jewellery that depended less on expensive stones in flamboyant settings and more on the use of unusual semiprecious gems, combined with inexpensive material such as horn. Lalique's dragonfly tiara comb from 1903–4, pictured top, combines horn, cast glass, enamelled gold and fire opals, while Wolfers uses an understated pastel palette in a pendant with a mythological theme, pictured below.

LEFT Orchids fascinated the Art Nouveau designers with their erotic forms and delicate colours. The orchid hair ornament by Belgian jeweller Philippe Wolfers (circa 1905–7) is made from gold with *plique-à-jour* enamelwork, accented with diamonds and rubies.

1910–19:
The Edwardian Era

While Art Nouveau attempted to evade retrospection in its style, striving for an ahistorical mystical modernity, many of the leading jewellery firms were looking backward to eighteenth-century French Rococo for their motifs. Rococo was a style that was intimately connected with the French courts at Versailles, its name derived from *rocaille*, or "rocks", specifically the small rock or shell formations found in grottoes. In design terms it meant delicacy, elegance and a profusion of gilding applied to feminine forms derived from nature – a light, dexterous style that can be seen at its most accomplished in the paintings of court favourites François Boucher (1703–70) and Jean-Honoré Fragonard (1732–1806).

The Rococo Revival style was the one that announced wealth and social status, perfect for a newly emerging middle-class of industrialists, entrepreneurs and bankers who loved the symbolic association with the great royal dynasties of the past. Mrs Cornelius Vanderbilt was but one member of many American families who attempted to channel the pomp and splendour of Versailles into the salons of New York, taking her place in society in the guise of a modern Madame de Pompadour. She bought many of her jewels from Cartier, the popularizer of the Rococo Revival look. The firm specialized in eighteenth-century decorative motifs such as swag, bow, cartouche and wreath shapes, and many a gold tassel hung from brooches, collars and pendants. The use of the flower garland was so ubiquitous at Cartier that this type of early Edwardian jewellery is now referred to as the Garland style. Even to this day floral swags adorn the lids of Cartier's evocative red-and-gold boxes.

OPPOSITE The Edwardian period called for a heightened femininity in dress that was reminiscent of the Versailles court. The extreme décolletage of gowns led to an emphasis on jewellery for the neck and shoulders, such as sentimental lockets, velvet chokers and pendants.

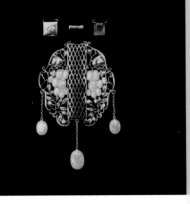

▲ Lavalier

The lavalier was a rather delicately constructed necklace popular in the Edwardian period and made up of several linked components set with gemstones in a trellis. The name is said to derive from Louise La Vallière, a celebrated mistress of Louis IV. This one is fashioned from gold and opals by the Wiener Werkstätte, circa 1915.

▶ Bandeaus and aigrettes

Popularized by couturier Paul Poiret, the evening bandeau in the Edwardian era had an attached aigrette, a jewelled hair ornament that included the feathers of the egret in the manner of a maharajah's turban. In and out of fashion since the seventeenth century, the aigrette appears in military ceremonial dress today.

Key looks of the decade
1910– 19

◀ Tiaras and headpieces

A heavily jewelled headpiece attributed to Charles Riffault for Boucheron. Riffault was a master of gold openwork and revived the technique of unbacked or translucent *cloisonné* enamelling.

Bows and swags

The graceful bow and swag designs first used in the late eighteenth century became a recognizable feature of Edwardian design appearing in earrings, pendants and brooches. Also the simple circular brooch, often representing a wreath or garland, is typical of the period.

Colliers de chien

Chokers, known as *colliers de chien* or dog collars, first became popular in Edwardian times in emulation of Queen Alexandra, who is said to have worn multiple rows of close-fiting pearls to conceal a scar on her neck. They usually comprise of several rows of pearls or a wide ribbon decorated with gemstones or brooches.

◀ Cameos

The cameo enjoyed a fresh wave of popularity. The most coveted were carved out of shell with the outer layers cut away to leave the design in relief against the darker background. The cameo was then set in a silver, gold or base metal frame. Many of the rarest are carved in Italy from volcanic lava.

▼ Garland necklace

A garland necklace is shorter than a standard necklace length, thus sits closer to the neck, and is decorated with a series of ornamental drops or pendants. The upswept hairstyles of the early 1900s laid emphasis upon the neck, which became an important area for the display of jewellery.

▲ White on white

The white on white style dominated fine jewellery, with silver and platinum settings taking over from gold. The style is most associated with Cartier, whose "invisible" settings made diamonds appear as if they were floating over the surface of the skin.

I920s:
Streamlined and Chic

Modernism transformed the look of the twentieth century arising like a phoenix from the ashes of the First World War to sweep away both the febrile swirls of Art Nouveau and the Rococo tracery of High Edwardian style. The first generation born in the twentieth century felt a deep-seated need to reject the cult of the past and the revivalist styles of jewellery that they associated with their parents. Modernism was clearly the appropriate aesthetic for the age of the machine: hard-edged, clean-cut and pared down to purity.

Such innovation of line and form first surfaced in the architecture of Adolf Loos in Vienna and Le Corbusier in France. Loos was garrulous in his antipathy to any overly decorative form in design, intoning, "Ornament is Crime" in his polemical writings. He continued, "We are approaching a new and greater time. No longer by an appeal to sensuality, but rather by economic dependence earned through work, will women bring about her equal status with man. Then velvet, silk and ribbons, feathers and paint will fail to have their effect. They will disappear."

Fashion did indeed undergo a transformation, but perhaps not as radically as Loos would have liked, and the more youthful streamlined *garçonne* silhouette – with its dropped waist, perfect for showing off long strings of beads, sleeveless shift dresses and shortened skirts – reflected the new opportunities for women that were emerging professionally, socially and politically. The new woman or "flapper", as the popular press dubbed her, had hair newly bobbed or shorn into an Eton crop, all the better for showing off a pair of huge drop earrings in ivory or Cubist cloisonné. Such "bright young things" made the old sartorial rules redundant; softly dimpled faces no longer flirted behind fans but were vividly painted, scarlet red lips drawn into a Cupid's bow amid lashings of stark white face powder. Socialite and novelist Violet Trefusis, daughter of Alice Keppel (the mistress of Edward VII) and lover of Vita Sackville-West, wrote of the new "brittle" goddesses with "bones of joss sticks, eyes by Fabergé and hearts made out of Venetian glass" such as the fictitious character Terpsichore van Pusch, who wore "a hat with two little mercury wings specifically designed for her by Lucienne" with matching diamond wings on her ears.

OPPOSITE A Cartier necklace and matching earrings in emeralds and pearls create Modernist elegance in 1924. The Art Deco dress pin and cabochon headband were re-interpreted by many fine and costume jewellers.

Egyptian and ethnic motifs
Inspiration came from Oriental, Indian and Egyptian art. Following Howard Carter's discovery of Tutankhamen's tomb and artefacts in 1922, Egyptian motifs became all the rage.

▼ Bangles and cuff bracelets
Silent-screen star Olga Baclanova, aka the "Russian Tigress", models the cuff bracelet, a popular jewellery design in the 1920s. The cuff could be simple when moulded in Perspex; avant-garde and "barbaric" when sported in armfuls or the height of luxury when fashioned out of gold and studded with diamonds.

Key looks of the decade
1920s

▲ Venetian beads
Beads enjoyed a vogue as they could be produced in a variety of vivid colours and intricate designs. Venetian beads incorporated floral features that today are prized by collectors all over the world. They are created by heating and stretching glass rods, which are then thinly sliced and moulded into beads.

▼ Art Deco
Many women wore fan-shaped Spanish-style hair combs as not everyone had a bob in the 1920s. The fan, together with the chevron, was one of the most popular motifs of this period and appears in architecture and interior as well as jewellery design. These celluloid combs from the mid 1920s are outlined in blue and green rhinestones.

▼ Tasselled necklaces

Long necklaces made of glass beads and ending in a tassel, originally called sautoirs, were re-named "flapper beads". They were accompanied by tassel earrings that dangled below newly shorn bobbed hair and tasselled shimmy dresses that created an energetic sense of movement when participating in new dance crazes like the Charleston.

Machine-cut gemstones

High-quality cutting and polishing with the aid of machines took over from the traditional hand work. This meant that more facets and complicated new cuts could be introduced. Plastic also suited the new mechanical processes and was available in a wide variety of colours and finishes.

▲ Geometric settings

Edwardian floral designs seemed desperately outmoded to a new generation of young women who were forging ahead to find their place in a modern post-war world. The *garçonne* look of the 1920s needed a new kind of jewellery to match and geometric settings held sway, as in this diadem and collar by Cartier from 1926.

◀ Glass and crystal

Combined with silver, glass and crystal was a combination that could achieve sparkling effects when matched with beaded flapper dresses. Here a silver necklace is given a visual lift with the insertion of carved red glass tablets.

THIS PAGE The romance of the machine and the speed and dynamism of modern metropolitan life was reflected in 1920s jewellery design. A ring by Alexandre Marchak of Paris, circa 1920–30, combines platinum with coral, diamonds and innovative black plastic, right, while a gold and chrome ring set with diamonds by Jean Desprès, circa 1930, is achieved in the ball-bearing style, below.

The Machine Aesthetic

The important jewellers associated with French Art Deco include Jean Fouquet, Gérard Sandoz, Suzanne Belperron and Raymond Templier – all of whose work experimented with the basic geometry of circles, the smooth surfaces of squares and sharp-edged rectangles reflecting the general vogue for what design historian Bevis Hillier dubbed "domesticated Cubism". Raymond Templier made full use of the chevron, a particularly popular shape in Art Deco jewellery, having originally appeared on the canvases of the Italian Futurists who were operating as an avant-garde group in the cities of Milan and Turin just before the First World War.

Speed transfixed these Italian mavericks, conveyed pictorially by the use of sequenced diagonals, planes, angles and interpenetrating forms. Artist Giacomo Balla, in particular, used the chevron to convey a sense of wonder at the technology that was changing the world, such as the 1909 electrification of Milan in "Street Light" (1909–10), a painting in which multicoloured chevrons are used to depict the dynamism of a street lamp's cosmic glow. The machine aesthetic can also be seen in the paintings of Tamara de Lempicka, who painted a self-portrait in 1929 that is the epitome of Art Deco glamour: the artist as a heavy-lidded Russian émigré posed in a shiny green Bugatti racing car with leather gloves, a metallic leather driving cap

and a billowing scarf. The perfect woman for Jean Fouquet, for instance, who began to design bulkier rings in the 1920s using frosted rock crystal, cabochon moonstones and faceted amethysts set into platinum, correctly believing that "the female hand holding the steering wheel would not be able to adorn itself with too fragile a ring".

This glamorous modern woman would surely have been the customer for the most extreme examples of machine-inspired style such as the jewellery constructed out of ball bearings by Charlotte Perriand, Jean Després and Gérard Sandoz. Ball bearings were commonly used to eliminate friction in mechanical parts, specifically axles, and took the form of simple chromium-plated brass balls – a fabulous shape for invention. These perfect silver spheres were threaded onto lengths of steel or copper wire to make the most Modernist of necklaces and sautoirs (a type of long necklace with a pendant or tassel hanging from the end) or were trapped between cases of ebonite and displayed on the arm. It would have taken a woman of great presence to wear this kind of jewellery when her contemporaries complacently flashed their diamonds. In 1920, film star and celebrated bisexual Marlene Dietrich was spotted in a silver bracelet created by Cartier that was decorated with small gold spheres in the ball-bearing style – reputedly a present from her lover, Jean Gabin.

BELOW LEFT An enamelled and lacquered silver cigarette case by Art Deco jeweller Gérard Sandoz takes the dynamic angles of Futurism and converts them into an *objet de luxe*.

BELOW RIGHT Raymond Templier channels the vocabulary of a working engine to fashion a stunning brooch out of white gold, brilliant-cut diamonds, onyx and coral, circa 1930.

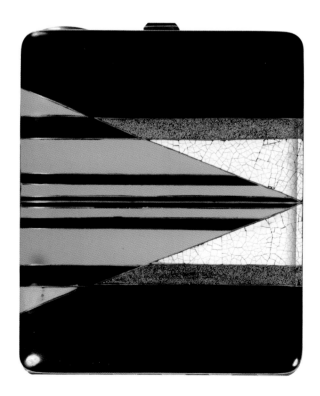

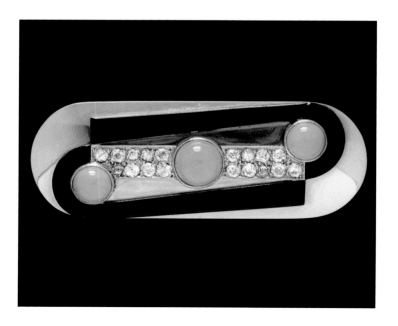

1930s:
Hollywood Glamour

Panic hit the world as the American Stock Market collapsed in 1929 after years of unscrupulous gambling by banks, corporations and city financiers. An economic slump followed, dubbed the Great Depression, which lasted until the end of the 1930s and affected the lives of most people in the Western world. The sudden disappearance of the rich American consumer caused great concern in the luxury industries; Cartier immediately sent employees across the Atlantic to pick up any pieces that had not yet been paid for and Coco Chanel dramatically halved her prices.

The silver screen gave much-needed respite in such troubled times and created a hunger for glamour among the consumer, as people dreamed of a better time to come. Established fashion houses soon found that their monopoly was being usurped by film stars, who became the new celebrities – their every moment documented in the pages of fan magazines. The fashionable silhouette moved away from the androgynous *garçonne* to a more womanly voluptuousness and clothes were cut in the round to cling to every curve, a style popularized by Madeleine Vionnet in Paris and on screen by Jean Harlow. The star's platinum blonde hair and white satin gowns inspired a vogue for "blondeness". Interior designer Syrie Maugham had a house with white walls, white satin curtains, white velvet lampshades and white lilies in white vases. Accordingly the "white on white" style made a spectacular comeback in jewellery design re-marketed as *le note blanche* and white gold and platinum became the favoured metals used in Art Deco designs. Gems were there to sparkle above all, offering up prisms of light to catch the eye – an aesthetic that was effortlessly effective when captured on black and white film. The camera lingered over every glint and glitter seeming to absorb the white heat of every shard of "ice" including Harlow's infamous diamond-studded cigarette holder in *Public Enemy* (1931).

The coming of sound to the movies also led to a dramatic change in jewellery. Heavy beads and clattering bangles that added exotic drama to the theatrical gesturing of the silent film had no place on the sound stage. Designers experimented with rubber jewels to little effect and simply turned to tighter-fitting necklace and bracelet styles. This new aesthetic was readily noted and copied by an adoring audience.

OPPOSITE In the 1930s a Hollywood-inspired glamour was evoked in jewellery editorial. Gems were there to sparkle, as in this photograph by Horst P Horst of 1939.

▶ Diamonds

Due to the advertising efforts of the diamond merchants, diamond sales increased 55 per cent. This diamond and ruby bow brooch, part of the Duchess of Windsor's personal collection, was sold in 1987. Many of her 1930s pieces were designed by Suzanne Belperron, Van Cleef & Arpels, Cartier and Harry Winston.

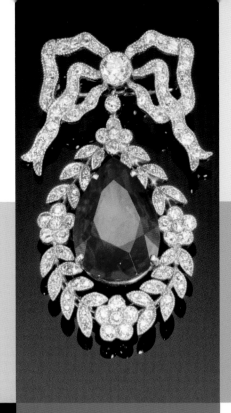

Stepped motifs and circles

The geometric forms of Modernism remained popular in the 1930s and found their way into jewellery of every price range – stepped motifs, chevrons and circles are typical of this decade's mainstream production.

Key looks of the decade
1930s

▼ Floral motifs

Flower motifs came back into fashion, but this time they were streamlined and stylized rather than overtly figurative. This fashion illustration from 1931 depicts a platinum necklace and matching brooch by Mauboussin in the form of exotic orchids in enamel set with diamonds.

▲ Filigree settings

Gold- and silverplated sterling, often combined with crystal gems, formed filigree settings for showy pieces, the best-known of which were by Hobé. Here a 1930s French gold-coloured filigree brooch features blue rhinestone glass jewels.

▶ Dime Store Deco

This term is used to define the kind of jewellery that would have been bought in the five-and-ten stores that were a major sector of American retailing by the 1930s, the best known being Woolworths. The motifs of the prevailing fashion were provided in cheap and cheerful examples, such as this Deco-inspired buckle and button set.

◀ White on white

American actress Irene Dunne shows off a diamond bracelet in the "white on white" style, circa 1935. This glossy luxe look was a popular trend in both jewellery and Hollywood set design, where white fur mixed with diamonds and marabou perfectly fitted the monochromatic demands of black-and-white film.

Flashy fakes

Whether real or faux, jewellery in every price range became distinctly flashy in the 1930s. Fine stones were brilliantly cut to give as much fire as possible and costume jewellery followed the same sparkling aesthetic.

▲ Dress clips

Popular from the late 1920s to the 1950s, dress clips are a good starting point for any budding collector. Most manufacturers of costume jewellery in the 1930s made them as their price suited Depression incomes and their versatility meant they could add interest to any outfit. Some were mounted in frames so as to be worn together as a single brooch.

LEFT An illustration from the 1931 edition of *The Delineator*, a popular American women's magazine that was published from 1873 until 1937. It provided in-depth coverage of contemporary fashion with tips on how women could achieve the latest looks. This editorial shows how wearing many jewellery items at once was acceptable in the 1930s.

BELOW LEFT A dress clip and brooch combination, called a "Duette pin", is fashioned in clear round and emerald square-cut rhinestones. The innovatory design mechanism, attributed to Coro, allows dress clips to slide into a pin from the sides, latching with a pushdown tab.

BELOW A Czechoslovakian glass bead, celluloid and rhinestone necklace shows why Czech craftsmen have enjoyed a reputation for high-quality glass jewellery since the late nineteenth century. Settings are usually of yellow metal alloy.

ABOVE A spectacular pair of Moderne collars from the 1930s shows how French Art Deco became big, bold and glamorous during the Hollywood years. On the left French jet and paste are combined to create a glittering monochromatic effect and on the right raw and enamelled steel links end in a dangling triangular pendant of green glass.

RIGHT A pair of early, circa 1940, Trifari fur clips feature a Hollywood-style Baroque leaf and flower design entwined with a navy blue enamel ribbon.

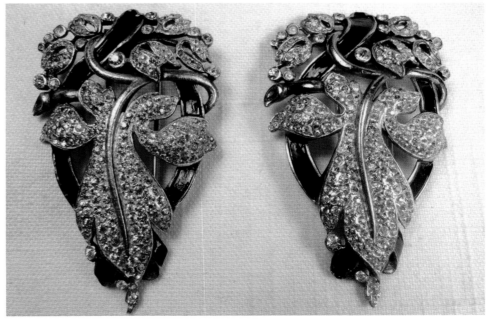

1940s:
F for Fake

In a world of war, costume jewellery was an important boost for feminine morale when fashion was under ration and austerity held sway. As clothes became increasingly utilitarian to fit the austere mood, costume jewellery was the perfect antidote – it could "jolly up" any amount of tweed. Jewellery production slowed right down in Europe and widespread bombing decimated important manufacturing centres such as Birmingham in England and Pforzheim in Germany. Paris, although occupied, had a wealthy audience and its prestigious firms kept going despite a lack of materials. Many pieces of unwanted jewellery were broken up and reset, and the market for antique jewellery expanded.

Patriotic jewellery boosted the spirit both at home and abroad with red, white and blue being a symbolic and emotional combination, the colours of both the American Stars and Stripes and the Union Jack. As Austrian Swarovski crystals became harder to source, companies found ingenious ways to give showy effects to their jewellery lines such as using polished Lucite instead of gemstones.

Platinum was an impossibility as it was essential for the production of armaments, so gold became the principal precious metal, albeit lighter, thinner sheets. Large brooches were popular but many were hollow inside and the snake or gas-pipe chain, a sinuously ribbed flexible gold tube, became the height of fashion. For those who could not afford pure gold, vast quantities of sterling silver were gold plated to create vermeil, which was easily mistaken for the real thing. This idea of plating silver with gold was not new; in fact, it dates back to the eighteenth century when jewellers applied mercury and gold to silver and then exposed it to extreme heat. As the mercury vaporized, the gold adhered to the silver, although the toxic fumes caused artisans to lose their sight – the technique was banned by the nineteenth century. Gold vermeil in the 1940s was produced using the electrolytic process.

Taking a lead from Chanel, the whole nature of fake changed; it glorified in the artificial – no real gem could assume such gigantic proportions. Plastic became completely acceptable as a malleable material that could assume any form a confident woman was prepared to wear; it was moulded into Scottie dogs, cowboys with lassos, huge necklaces of bright berries or dancing harlequins.

OPPOSITE Marvella was a brand of costume jewellery founded by New York businessman Sol Weinreich, in 1906. The company specialized in simulated pearls so highly regarded that this set comprising a brooch, necklace and bracelet was featured in *Vogue* in 1945.

Metal and wood

The war led to shortages of precious materials, so designers looked elsewhere for inspiration. This Italian necklace and brooch, 1942–5, have been fashioned from a combination of metal and wood. Italian designers, such as Salvatore Ferragamo, led the way in this type of fashion experimentation.

Surrealism

One of the key Surrealist themes, natural forms were explored because of their symbolism and structural beauty. Along with Dalí, Verdura and Schiaparelli, there were biomorphic shapes from Calder, Kramer and de Patta.

▲ Jelly Belly

A design for a swan pin with a baroque pearl by Fulco di Verdura, circa 1940. This is a deluxe example of the popular Jelly Belly style that is associated with Alfred Philippe at Trifari. Jelly Bellies were manufactured in myriad of figurative forms with Lucite "bellies" set into silver- or gold-plated settings.

▼ Rhinestones

Rhinestones, a faceted stone made of glass to imitate diamonds, featured heavily in 1940s jewellery, particularly those made in Providence, Rhode Island – the centre of American costume jewellery production. The cheapness of this artificial gem meant that women could copy the razzle-dazzle they saw in the cinema.

Key looks of the decade
1940s

Patriotic pins

Flags, stars, military motifs, souvenir and sweetheart themes in the popular red, white and blue all found their way into 1940s jewellery, especially those crafted with Bakelite, metalwork or enamelling.

▶ Sterling silver

As a result of the lack of precious materials during the war, sterling silver increased in popularity as it was one of the few precious materials allowed for use in costume jewellery. A high-grade alloy, sterling silver contains a minimum of 92.5 per cent silver and 7.5 per cent of another metal, usually copper.

◤ Floral motifs

The geometry of Art Deco, which had dominated jewellery production in the inter-war years, was taken over by stylized floral motifs in the 1940s. A neo-Victorian nostalgia was unleashed by the threat of war, and women who were operating under rigorous conditions sought a dreamy romance in their jewellery with added rhinestone glitz.

▲ Vermeil

Derived from the French word for "veneer", vermeil is also known as silver gilt. The process involves coating sterling silver with a thin gold plating by electrolysis to give the impression of being solid gold. This clip brooch is vermeil with semiprecious stones, fretwork and snakelink hangings.

▲ Fine jewellery

Fine jewellery was as elaborate as costume jewellery; sometimes the two were difficult to tell apart. Firms like Hobé even used real gems among artificial ones in their work. Here, actress Meg Mundy is wearing a set of cabochon emeralds and diamonds.

Miriam Haskell

American costume jeweller Miriam Haskell (1899–1981), whose firm still exists today, was born in Albany, Indiana, in 1899, one of four children. She began designing and producing jewellery in 1924 and opened her first boutique, Le Bijou de l'Heure, in 1926 in the McAlpin Hotel, New York City. Here she showed collections that owed more to the legacy of Art Nouveau than Art Deco; their motifs derived from nature rather than the machine, and asymmetry over geometry is the key design feature.

Haskell *bijouterie* was bought by some of the leading lights of New York's fashionable scene. Customers included film stars Joan Crawford, who was reputed to have several pieces from every Haskell season; Lucille Ball, who regularly flew out from Los Angeles for a private showing of the latest looks; and the coolly elegant Duchess of Windsor, through whom she was introduced to Coco Chanel. The French couturier and the American designer were both independent, free-spirited women of means in the competitive world of fashion and struck up a firm friendship, gossiping over coffee as they sourced fabulous blown-glass Murano beads at their favourite Maison Gripoix.

Together with head designer Frank Hess, with whom she worked until his retirement in 1960, Haskell created costume jewellery of understated beauty and meticulous detail. Every Venetian bead, Bohemian crystal and faux baroque pearl was handwired to intricate brass filigree and then backed to a second filigree to conceal any trace of its construction. Beads were then worked up into three dimensions to create textural layers, held together with soft honey-toned metal filigree wiring. As a result one piece may have taken as long as three days to create, a lifetime in the world of costume jewellery and reflected in the occasionally prohibitive cost of each piece.

The advent of the Second World War forced Haskell to use alternative materials including plastics, beads, shell and crystals – all sourced a little closer to home. Later, in the early 1950s, Haskell designs became increasingly elaborate and showy as women wanted a more obvious glamour in their lives after the deprivations of war. Trinkets from this period include a pair of flamboyant Gauguin-inspired hibiscus earrings in painted porcelain and gold, and flashing stickpins of a style that can only be described as Hollywood Baroque. Huge necklaces had strands of multiple crystal beads separated by Japanese pearls, coral or huge gold-tone leaves, while brooches were set with a multitude of stones, pearls and tiny glass seed-beads in shades of aqua, robin's egg blue and pastel pink.

BELOW A Miriam Haskell and Frank Hess grand parure, with accompanying original artwork (bottom centre) by Larry Austin. The pink set comprises a three-strand bracelet, three dress clips and a necklace.

BELOW LEFT AND RIGHT Original watercolour artworks by Larry Austin promoting the Haskell parures pictured opposite, top left and below.

COLLECTING MIRIAM HASKELL

* Because all pieces are handmade, they are quite fragile and difficult to restore.
* Unmarked until 1947, work was stamped with her name on a horseshoe cartouche, an oval stamp, and on the hook or clasp.
* Early unsigned necklaces tend to have elaborate box clasps; later signed pieces use a distinctive adjustable hook and tail.
* A good way to identify an authentic Haskell is by vintage ads, such as those opposite.
* Nearly all have a pierced metal (pre-1943), plastic (during war years) or filigree plate (postwar) onto which the decorative details were attached. Mesh was never used.

TOP LEFT A Haskell and Hess parure, including a bracelet, brooch and three clips of goldstone nasturtium leaves.

TOP RIGHT An unsigned 1940 parure attributed to Miriam Haskell featuring poured glass pink and lavender petals.

FAR LEFT A 1940 parure by Haskell and Hess, including a lariat wrap necklace of aqua glass beads with silver-tone leaves decorated with rhinestone pavé, a necklace of aqua glass bead balls and clear rhinestone leaves and a four-strand bracelet.

1950s:
Mid-Century Sparkle

After years of war, the doors of Paris were open at last; couture houses were in full swing again and women, hungering after new looks, waited with breathless anticipation to see where style would go next. They didn't have to wait too long – in 1947 the world woke up to a fashion revolution. In couturier Christian Dior's Paris atelier an enraptured audience was introduced to a new grown-up glamour: Dior's Corolle line, so-called because he wanted women to appear like the corolla (petals) of a flower. He gave his clients clothes that made their bodies emerge as if from a sea of silk and satin petals; tailoring was tight, waists waspie and the look was decadently deluxe. After years of scrimping and saving, making do and mending, women welcomed the retrospective romanticism of Dior's New Look, as it was dubbed by fashion magazine *Harper's Bazaar*, with open arms.

Yellow gold was still popular, this time with a textured surface and set with gems in colour combinations of turquoise and coral or amethyst and pearl that deliberately quoted the seasonal palettes of the inventive French couturiers – although diamonds were still women's stone of choice. In fact, pearls enjoyed something of a renaissance, their ladylike appeal, when worn by the patrician Grace Kelly, given a modern kick in new shades of champagne, coffee and mink.

Modernism kept running alongside all this frippery; this time the influence was from Scandinavia, whose designers introduced a soft, organic version, seen to its best expression in the designs of silversmith Georg Jensen. Abstract forms associated with what was known as the "Atomic Age" ran rampant in textile design, interiors and jewellery, providing a fresh source of inspiration in the post-war world. Starbursts, biomorphic shapes and molecular structures were rendered in diamonds by the most prestigious firms, or in copper and ceramics on the high street.

OPPOSITE A model wearing jewellery by Schreiner in 1957. Schreiner was a costume jewellery company, based in New York and known for its use of "keystone" or overly long baguette stones. The company collaborated with many American fashion designers in the 1950s.

▼ Florals and natural themes

Nature remained a popular theme for both fine and costume jewellery, but the Scandinavian designers understood the spiritual and elemental qualities of the natural world and presented it in a more abstract way. This Hattie Carnegie leaf and berry brooch is typical of the mainstream floral look of the period.

Chandelier earrings

The decade's shorter hair fashions changed the focus to the earlobe, with long drop earrings becoming fashionable. Oversized shoulder-skimming styles were possible due to lighter settings and faux gemstones.

▲ Beads

The 1950s was a decade of colour, after the drab khakis of wartime uniform. Palettes were strong and vibrant, and fashion followed suit. This Miriam Haskell necklace of banana yellow shows how the work of this company adapted to the 1950s zeitgeist.

▶ Textured gold

Yellow gold remained popular, but was given a contemporary twist with the application of a textured surface. This wide, basket-weave, hinged bracelet, 1955, is by Hattie Carnegie, a New York fashion entrepreneur who created her own lines of ready-to-wear and costume jewellery.

▲ Scandinavian Modern

With its emphasis on natural materials, Scandinavian Modern was a breath of fresh air. Kalevala Koru, the largest manufacturer in Finland, was founded in 1937 and, like other Scandinavian firms, based its design aesthetic on vernacular culture and nature, like this ring from 1959.

Key looks of the decade
1950s

▶ Figurative brooches

The whimsical jewellery that cheered up the drab fashions of the 1940s remained popular, while the increase in foreign travel meant that global culture was plundered for motifs. Countries were rendered in clichés – the Eiffel Tower stood for France and a diamanté-encrusted sombrero for Mexico.

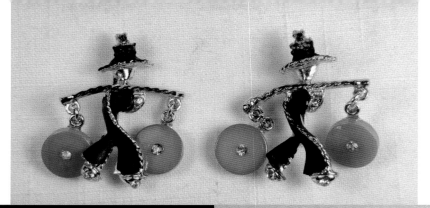

▼ Parures

A parure is the name for a suite of jewellery designed to be worn all at the same time such as a necklace, bracelet and earrings. This early 1950s parure by Weiss features sparkling navette and chaton stones. The company was known for floral and figurative designs featuring carefully colour-coordinated, Austrian rhinestones.

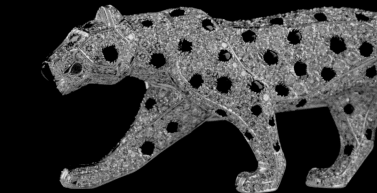

▲ Luxury jewellery

After the impasse of war the prestigious jewellery houses returned to producing incredible work that fitted in with the deluxe couture look, such as this iconic panthère brooch in platinum by Cartier, encrusted with 511 diamonds, 72 onyx spots, and emerald eyes.

▲ Copper jewellery

Renoir of California, founded in 1946 by Jerry Fels, produced copper jewellery until the mid 1960s and the Matisse mark was used on a series of enamelled pieces that were produced from the early 1950s. These 1950s Renoir Matisse pieces take the form of autumn leaves accented with red enamel.

◀ Pearls

The 1950s was the era of pearls; natural, culture or faux, and they appeared on every type of jewellery throughout the decade. Gold-tone pieces accented with huge faux pearls, like this Trifari pin and clip earrings with pearl, were used to accent simple tailored suits by day.

Charm bracelets

By the 1950s, the charm bracelet was the must-have accessory, with a new link to record each rite of passage and interest, from birthdays and anniversaries to hobbies and travel. Today some of these vintage bracelets sell for remarkably high prices at auction.

1960s:
POP Goes the Future

The 1960s was a decade that looked to the future with optimism; culture was harnessing the "white heat of new technology", stated British Prime Minister Harold Wilson, whose prophetic words went on to define the key characteristics of the era. The structured silhouette of 1950s couture and the voluptuous curves of the Hollywood bombshell disappeared to be replaced by a new ideal – the androgynous, pre-adolescent figure exemplified by London model Twiggy. Her sporty, futuristic, even anti-maternal image and pared-down geometric clothes made 1950s fashion look too prim, too grown-up – just too plain old.

Fashion was no longer aimed at the privileged elite. Parisian designers lost their hold on the market with the death of Christian Dior in 1957, as the fashionable silhouette took its influence from London and the emerging Mod scene. Excessive grooming and ladylike primness were cast aside in the rush for liberation by postwar baby-boomers newly defined as "teenagers". Adolescence was infinitely extendable, it seemed, as the young became more financially independent and rejected parental control – it was everything to be young.

Italian style emerged as France's successor, with names such as Gucci, Pucci and Ferragamo signifying youthful cool. In London, Mary Quant designs sparked a sartorial revolution and were positioned as the fashion equivalent of the Beatles. Any intimation of adulthood in dress was rejected; hats, gloves and handbags were incongruous in a decade of miniskirts, Sassoon bobs and knee-length boots. Precious jewellery was worn in a more insouciant way and many women bought into the idea that too much high-end jewellery could be ageing.

The bangle became a perfect medium to convey the 1960s futuristic motifs. Oversize accessories in saturated colour or Space-Age metallic referenced the work of artists such as Frank Stella and Bridget Riley, who provided a fertile seam of inspiration. Images of the Op and Pop artists – stripes, targets and optically challenging black and white – were incorporated into high-street and high-end jewellery. Scandinavian jewellery retained its "arty" reputation and designers such as Finnish duo Timo and Pentti Sarpaneva and Björn Weckström sought inspiration from their native landscape using textured bronze, indigenous stones such as quartz and gold nuggets from Lapland. David-Anderson settled back into the Norwegian company's trademark aesthetic of restrained simplicity and stated, "We view with a measure of scepticism those aspects of design which are considered high fashion and which rely for their effect on the sensational."

OPPOSITE In a new decade of optimism, bright saturated colour entered design inspired by Pop Art and American abstract painters such as Frank Stella. A model in 1966 wears a tomato-coloured linen dress with geometric neckline by B H Wragge and enormous clip-on abstract earrings.

▶ Black is Beautiful

The Black is Beautiful movement of the late 1960s led to the vogue among young black people for fashion that expressed their cultural and historical identity. Natural hair was grown into an Afro rather than pressed straight and a more Afro-centric style included huge beaded collars and bib necklaces.

Revival jewellery

Victorian Revival-style came back for a short time, with jewellery that took the form of plastic and resin cameos, such as the collectable Gerry's and Juliana cameos, as well as engraved and antiqued metalwork buckles and bangles.

Key looks
of the decade
1960s

▼ Space Age

A Paco Rabanne dress made up of linked plastic squares from April 1967. Rabanne made his name in the 1960s with a series of futuristic garments. When viewed on the catwalk they appeared to be Space-Age prototypes rather than high fashion.

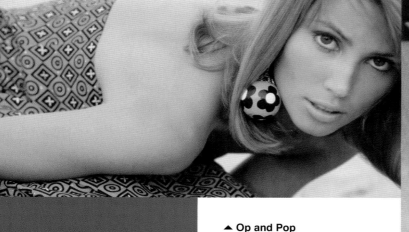

▲ Op and Pop

Geometric effects were a simple way of making jewellery modern and were influenced by the Op Art paintings of Bridget Riley and Victor Vasarely. A model wears a navy and orange cotton wrap by Gayle Kirkpatrick for Atelier with oversized drop earrings with the ever-popular daisy motif from Tree House in 1966.

◀ Zingy colours

The 1960s were the decade of bright primary colour, as seen in this enamel butterfly pin by Trifari. The work of Pop artists such as Andy Warhol and Roy Lichtenstein used the visual language of popular rather than high culture and bright hard-edged graphics found their way into all areas of art and design, including jewellery.

▶ Hippie motifs

"Flower power" was a term originally coined by Beat poet Allen Ginsberg in the late 1960s as a call to peaceful anti-Vietnam demonstrations and passive rather than violent resistance. Hippies adopted the flower as decorative motif and it entered mainstream fashion jewellery.

◀ Pendants

Huge pendants became fashionable and continued to be so in the 1970s. Most costume jewellery manufacturers like Sarah Coventry and Goldette through to upmarket silversmiths like David Andersen, produced them. Shapes included articulated animals such as owls, ethnic motifs and the ubiquitous Maltese cross.

Ethnic trends

Interpretations of East Indian, Egyptian and Asian looks worked their way into jewellery design, often with combinations of one or more ethnic elements. These styles, which carried on into the 1970s, often used bold, colourful jewels such as in the creations of Kenneth Jay Lane, Accessocraft, Trifari and Goldette.

▲ Plastic

After the Space-Age experiments of designers such as Pierre Cardin, Courrèges, Pierre Cardin and Rudi Gernreich, plastic became a popular material, as seen in the furniture of Joe Columbo and bright plastic jewellery such as these Perspex rings from the mid 1960s.

Pop Plastic

The influence of Pop Art was paramount in the 1960s. The movement had its origins in the previous decade when artists Eduardo Paolozzi and Peter Blake found inspiration in the brightly coloured visual language of popular culture rather than the introspective musings of Abstract Expressionism. In New York Andy Warhol was painting large-scale versions of supermarket products such as the Campbell's Soup Can series and Roy Lichtenstein copied the style of the comic strip. These paintings glorified the bright gaudy aesthetic of advertising and product design, and a new primary palette entered the world of design.

Richard Hamilton was one of the founders of the Pop Art movement in Britain and his collage work such as "Just What Is It That Makes Today's Homes So Different, So Appealing" reflects the postwar boom years when domestic products were freely available and imbued with glamour. Hamilton had a set of rules for the new art that ran: "[It should be] Popular (designed for a mass audience); transient (short-term solution); expendable (easily forgotten); low cost; mass-produced; young (aimed at youth); witty; sexy; gimmicky; glamorous; and last but not least, Big Business." The same principles were applied to the decade's jewellery design; much of it was cheap and cheerful, produced in huge quantities and with a built-in obsolescence – it was not meant to last. Materials such as plastics, particularly Perspex and vinyl, were moulded into chunky geometric shapes and coloured with primary hues by designers such as Raymond Exton. Partners David Watkins and Wendy Ramshaw took the notion of expendability to the extreme in their paper jewellery, which could be bought in kit form at Mary Quant's Bazaar and the Way In boutique on the top floor of Harrods, Knightsbridge, in the 1960s. Watkins said:

When we first designed paper jewellery back in the 1960s, we were motivated by our desire to use processes outside the mainstream of jewellery production. The idea of printing jewellery really appealed to us. We wanted to create things that were fast and simple and fun and inexpensive. And throwaway – the throwaway concept was intriguing at the time.

RIGHT A bright primary palette is one of the hallmarks of 1960s jewellery, reflecting the optimism of the post-war "baby boomer" generation. Plastics, seen as innovative and futuristic, were moulded into huge pieces of gaudy jewellery as in this huge neckpiece of 1967.

RIGHT Twiggy (real name Lesley Hornby) was a top model and style leader in this decade and together with the Beatles was responsible for importing the so-called "Swinging London" style into America. In 1965 she wears yellow plastic earrings with the daisy motif, as popularized by British designer Mary Quant.

BELOW A selection of 1960s enamel flower brooches. These huge colourful pins were one of the most popular jewellery forms of the decade, as they were a visual symbol of "flower power", a slogan used by the American hippie movement.

The Black and White of Colour

"Op Art" was first coined by *Time* magazine in 1964, which went on to describe the new art movement as "an attack on the eye". Artists such as Bridget Riley, Richard Anuszkiewicz and Victor Vasarely used perceptual research to create geometric patterns that produced dizzying visual effects in the viewer. Black-and-white canvases shimmered, shifted and flowed at the "Responsive Eye" exhibition held at New York's Museum of Modern Art in 1965 and although proclaimed "optical hysteria" by one critic, their influence quickly filtered through to fashion. American dress manufacturers like Larry Aldrich saw the potential of this bold monochromatic look and commissioned fabrics inspired by his own collection of Op Art paintings; in London Ossie Clark and John Bates created Op Art clothes for their hip clientele.

Op Art jewellery was a short-lived fad, designed quickly and cheaply to match the black-and-white clothes. Plastic could create stark checkerboard effects and was moulded into bangles, dangle earrings and bold bead necklaces. Target designs were popular in red and white, as well as in black, and became a motif of the burgeoning Mod movement that was to revive Carnaby Street as a fashionable destination and pinpoint London across the world as a new "swinging" capital of style. Mary Quant's iconic black-and-white daisy motif appeared on acrylic jewellery, although it was less Op and more personal in its significance. Quant relates how as a teenager she had fallen for an older man and wished his girlfriend dead. To the designer's horror she expired of appendicitis; her name, Daisy. The Op Art style may have been short-lived in its purest form but its effects lasted longer. Public taste started to swing to abstract rather than figurative forms in jewellery design and an innovative vocabulary of asymmetrical, splintered and minimalist shapes began to appear.

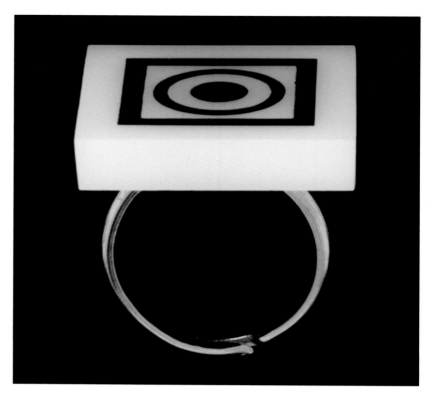

RIGHT (ABOVE AND BELOW) A selection of Op Art-inspired acrylic and metal jewellery by Wendy Ramshaw, originally a textile designer, and David Watkins, a sculptor and jazz musician. The couple made this range of Optik Art Jewellery from 1963 and it was sold through boutiques such as Mary Quant's Bazaar. Ramshaw used the technique of screen-printing onto sheets of acrylic instead of the more usual spray-painting; the acrylic was then cut up into small sections for the jewellery.

BELOW Actress Jill Haworth wears enamel earrings and bracelet by Giorgio di Sant'Angelo for Vendome in primary-coloured plastic, 1967. Sant'Angelo had a studio apprenticeship with Picasso, who urged him to experiment with new materials. He combined plastics such as Lucite in vibrant jewellery that was spotted by Diana Vreeland, who employed him as a stylist on American *Vogue*. Sant'Angelo became one of America's most important fashion designers.

1970s:
The Body,
Bold and Beautiful

Recession and protest dogged the early years of the 1970s as disillusionment set in on global culture – the hippie philosophy of "Make Love, Not War" was increasingly untenable in a post-nuclear world. Jewellery began to display spirituality rather than obvious wealth, for many believed that there was no room for vulgarity in such sombre global circumstances. Fashion reflected the same understated trend – the hippie look turned mainstream and clothes continued to make reference to "ethnic" origins in the form of kaftans, patchwork peasant skirts and cheesecloth shirts. In the heady world of international style, Yves Saint Laurent, Bill Gibb and Zandra Rhodes converted the counter-cultural garb of the hippie movement into the high-status fashion of "poverty deluxe" – or "radical chic" as writer Tom Wolfe dubbed the look in America. A similar strategy was taken in the design of high-end jewellery, with established houses adapting to ethnic influences and street style.

The rise of radical feminism underscored the fact that the demonstration and protest of the previous decade were to continue as Germaine Greer's compelling book *The Female Eunuch* (1970) would attest. In her heady polemic, the fashion system was systematically trashed in print as an example of women's oppression in a patriarchal culture. Greer saw the bounties of nature being plundered to decorate the "Eternal Feminine" to insidious effect: "the depths of the sea are ransacked for pearl and coral to deck her; the bowels of the earth are laid open that she might wear gold, sapphires, diamonds and rubies". Jewellery took a serious turn and became an art form, embodying earnest polemic about its very status in the world more akin to conceptual art rather than luxury and status, as seen in the work of Dutch jeweller Robert Smit and Czechoslovakian goldsmith Hubertus von Skal.

OPPOSITE A model wears a printed, georgette Japanese-inspired kimono over mauve pyjamas by Rafael and a large, leaf-emblazoned necklace.

▶ Stickpins

As flashy costume jewellery went out of fashion in the 1970s, more discreet pieces became mainstream. Stickpins enjoyed a vogue. Originally worn by men to hold a necktie or cravat in place, they were adopted by women and worn on the lapel of the jacket. This Givenchy version is typical of the period.

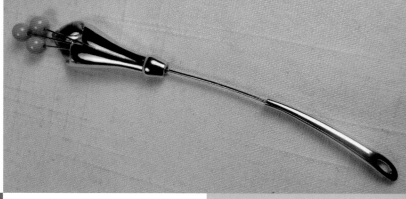

▶ Textured metal

Metal in all its forms dominated 1970s jewellery design. The absence of glittering stones forced designers to concentrate on textured surface effects and forms that were carved or moulded in relief. This Gilles Vidal pendant is typical of the influential work produced in Canada during this period.

Key looks of the decade
1970s

▲ Rope rings

As the fashion for sparkling gems declined, simpler rings in earth colours and natural materials, such as rosewood, ivory and ebony, took over and were worn in stacks on each hand. Here, the popular gold rope ring is mixed with others of cornelian, plain gold and chyrophase, a green-coloured chalcedony or quartz.

▶ Fashion jewellery

Costume jewellery relied more on the effects of metal than colourfully coordinated stones. This lariat tie necklace and earrings in gold-tone by Monet anticipates developments in the 1980s, when faux gold was the metal of choice. Monet, formerly Monocraft of 1928, was bought by Liz Claiborne in 2000.

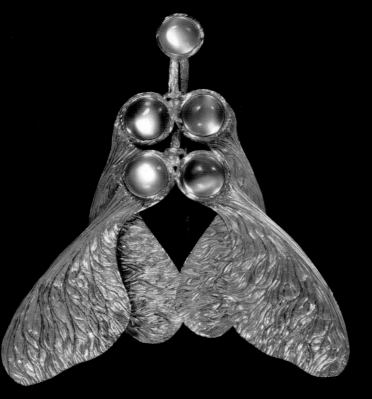

◀ **Art Nouveau Revival**

The continued influence of the hippie movement stimulated a craft revival and a re-awakening of interest in Art Nouveau. Malcolm Appleby – who continues to produce exquisite jewellery today – created this engraved gold brooch, taking the form of two sycamore wings with the seeds fashioned from moonstones, in 1975.

▲ **Body jewellery**

The sexual permissiveness of late 1960s hippie culture continued into the '70s with an increasing pre-occupation with the body. Jewellery began to take over from clothes as a way of fashioning the body, and designers from every level in the market produced their own versions. This Pierre Cardin collar dates from the early 1970s.

Bronze

In the 1970s, many designers, following the lead from Finnish jewellers such as Jorma Laine, began producing jewellery in bronze. A cheap alternative to gold, it was easy to cast and had a folksy feel. Tino and Pentti Sarpeneva used bronze in combination with amethyst and rose or smokey quartz.

▲ **Turquoise**

Silver and turquoise jewellery from Mexico and Arizona was especially fashionable in the early part of the 1970s. Its relationship with down-trodden cultures struck a chord with the Vietnam War generation. Cher, seen here in 1974, is part Cherokee and was regularly photographed in Native American jewellery.

1980s:
The Power and the Glory

The fashion experimentation of the late 1970s continued into the early years of the 1980s. Designers such as Vivienne Westwood, Jean Paul Gaultier and Franco Moschino worked with gender play and a plethora of historical references. Moschino, in particular, picked up where Elsa Schiaparelli had left off with Surrealist-inspired designs such as a quilted black denim mini with plastic fried eggs decorating the hemline, a jacket embellished with bottle tops, bodices made out of safety pins, and earrings fashioned from plug sockets.

The love of costume jewellery in all its forms reawakened interest in pieces from the past, which became immensely collectable. Original baubles, bangles and beads by earlier designers such as Hattie Carnegie, Joseff and Hobé began to increase in value and interest peaked when the first exhibition entirely devoted to costume jewellery, entitled "Jewels of Fantasy: Fashion Jewellery of the Twentieth Century", opened at the Museo Teatrale alla Scala in Milan in 1991. Visitors gawped at over 600 pieces by René Lalique, Elsa Schiaparelli, Miriam Haskell, Trifari and Christian Dior, among others, and the travelling show legitimized nonprecious jewellery as an art form worthy of worldwide recognition. American designer Robert Sorrell worked with the same spirit when he created handcrafted large-scale pieces in the manner of the Hollywood master-jewellers of the 1930s and 1940s in flashing Austrian crystal, pieces used by Thierry Mugler for his extravagant catwalk shows.

OPPOSITE Status jewellery was back with a vengeance in the 1980s, and exaggeration was a key aesthetic. These models are wearing jewellery by Stephen Dweck in 1985. The designer is known for his use of huge stones, such as Brazilian tourmalines, Australian boulder opals and South Sea pearls, for one-off pieces called OAK (One of a Kind).

▶ Gold and glitz

The 1980s trappings of luxurious excess included jewellery that was bold, brash and showy. The cult of visible wealth meant settings and stones, whether real or faux, had to be large and were a focal point for any elegant black dress.

Crucifixes

Maripol's original rosary-inspired designs, as famously worn by Madonna in the 1980s, became one of the defining looks of the decade and were produced by fashion houses such as Christian Lacroix, who created an elaborately designed version in rolled gold and on the high street.

Key looks of the decade
1980s

▼ Fluoros

Fluoro colours appeared as a counterpoint to the sophistication of gold and were influenced by post-punk and 1980s hip-hop. Lime green and pink, once seen in the graffiti art of New York's Keith Haring and the city's subways, crossed over into pieces such as this 1985 collar necklace by Steven Rosen.

▲ Bracelets and cuffs

The cuff bracelet made a comeback after the thin discreet metal bangle designs of the preceding decade. With its intimations of body armour, the thick metal cuff, studded with huge faux stones, matched the vogue for power dressing as women entered the executive workplace as the equals of men.

◀ Ropes and chains
The influence of punk could be seen in the exaggerated and almost fetishistic effects created by 1980s jewellery. Ropes and chains were worn in multiples by stars like Madonna (real name Madonna Louise Ciccone), whose influence was felt on the high street.

▼ Coin jewellery
The display of wealth through embellishment was at its most obvious with the revival of coin jewellery, one of the most ancient types of adornment. Bulgari, through Chanel, created coin jewellery for the high street. These 10-carat goldplated Chanel, quadrangle coin cluster earrings are typical of the decade.

▼ Geometrics
The geometry of Art Deco was revived and exaggerated on a much larger and dramatic scale. The elegance of Suzanne Belperron and Raymond Templier, pioneers of this aesthetic in the 1920s, was replaced with huge, abstract, gem-studded forms like this Yves Saint Laurent necklace and earrings.

Logos
The cult of visible wealth in the 1980s created a veritable logo-mania. Karl Lagerfeld was one of the most successful at this overt branding and transformed the House of Chanel from a rather matronly label into one of youthful energy and joie de vivre. Double "C" logos were fashioned into earrings, bracelets and pendants.

Shopping and Collecting Guide

Collecting vintage is the most sustainable way of consuming fashion – it's a perfect example of recycling and a key to creating your individual look. Stars of the past used jewellery to create a trademark: Gloria Swanson, grande dame of 1930s film, always sported a selection of thick, gold, slave cuffs on her left arm, while Audrey Hepburn was often seen wearing a bracelet of dangling charms. Interest in style icons such as these also has the effect of making such pieces increasingly collectable. Think of the future, too, as today's jewellery will be the vintage of the future: buy modern costume jewellery of quality, treat it with care and you will have heirlooms to pass down to your grandchildren.

The market for vintage jewellery remains buoyant and the key to buying well is quality and condition. Vintage costume jewellery by famous names such as Elsa Schiaparelli, Marcel Boucher and Miriam Haskell always holds its value and many fabulous pieces went unsigned, so bargains are still to be had. Look for corroded or worn plating, cloudy rhinestones, missing or cracked stones and chipped enamel. Though scratches in silver and gold can be repaired, blisters, cracks or holes cannot be restored. Fastenings should be tested to see if they still work effectively and avoid any pieces with obvious soldering because this probably means they have been repaired at some point.

Where to Buy

There are obvious outlets for buying vintage jewellery such as specialist jewellery fairs, retro fashion markets like Portobello Road and Bermondsey Market in London and the bustling flea markets of Clignacourt in Paris and Brooklyn, New York. Lille holds Europe's largest flea market during the first weekend of September. Along miles of pavement, two million stallholders lay out their wares – the atmosphere is amazing, with an incredible array of vintage jewellery at bargain prices. Charity and thrift shops can also be great for vintage jewellery and bargains are still to be had out there. Most major cities have a gem of a vintage jewellery store, such as Linda Bee, a long-established dealer in London's Grays Antique Market (who specializes in feline-related items), Miriam Haskell, Joseff of Hollywood and Schiaparelli. Pippin Vintage Jewellery in New York has baubles covering almost every inch of the store with prices ranging from $5 for kitsch costume jewellery to $800 for the finest antique pieces.

How to Spot Fake Costume Jewellery

As the demand for vintage costume jewellery has taken off, so many fakes have appeared on the market. One trick by some disreputable dealers is to amalgamate all the old rhinestones from broken pieces into a new setting. Vintage settings are usually smooth and rhodium plated; fakes may have a textured finish or an attempted "antiqued" or oxidized look. Genuine rhinestone jewellery must be at least 40 years old, so if the brooch you are perusing looks pristine, then it's probably new.

Check for any dust around the stones that could indicate age and look at the style of clasp – is it compatible with the date of the piece? Feel the weight of the jewellery and familiarize yourself with the trademark signatures and stamps of the key designers documented in this book. The American firm Weiss, for instance, always prong-set their stones, so if you see an item purporting to be Weiss and the stones are glued, you will recognize that it's a fake. Avoid more expensive pieces such as Trifari Jelly Bellies until you have developed your "eye" – remember it will be a process of trial and error at the start of your collecting bug. The best advice is to always question anything, particularly online, that looks like a real bargain – it most probably isn't. There are plenty of sites online providing information about specific styles, such as Miriam Haskell, that are being faked at any given moment (see http://imageevent.com/bluboi/haskellfakes), so be sure to do your homework before you make a bid.

Spotting a Fake Diamond

When buying a diamond bear in mind the four "Cs" – colour, cut, carat and clarity – and always go to a reputable dealer/appraiser if you intend to invest a lot of money. It is highly recommended that you obtain a certificate from the Gemological Institute of America (GIA). Generally speaking, the larger a diamond, the rarer it is; a 4-carat diamond is worth considerably more than two 2-carat diamonds of the same quality.

- Always pay great attention to the quality of the setting – a diamond is an expensive stone so the setting will never be in poor-quality metal.

- Real diamonds do not sparkle like rainbows; their light is grey and white.

- If the diamond is not in a setting, turn it upside down over a piece of newspaper. If you can easily read the print, it's a fake.

- Breathe over the diamond – the fog from your breath should disappear instantly. If it stays for more than two to three seconds, it's a fake.

- If a drop of water is put on the facet of a diamond it will remain a drop and not spread over the surface. If it does, the stone is glass or crystal.

OPPOSITE Model wears a two-piece blue blouse and skirt in the 1960s, accessorized with a coral bead necklace by David Webb. The beads are gathered together with gold and emerald cabochons.

Spotting a Fake Pearl

There are so many different kinds of pearl that identifying whether a pearl is real, cultured or fake can be a bit of a minefield. Even dealers have difficulties and it has been said that the only true test is to slice the pearl in half to see the layers of natural nacre or submit it to X-ray!

There are other less destructive or time-consuming ways to determine a real pearl from a fake, but they are by no means conclusive.

• Take the pearl and gently rub it over the surface of your teeth – a natural pearl should feel slightly gritty. Cultured pearls are a little smoother but should still retain a slight bumpy or gritty feel. Don't rush for your credit card yet, though, as fake pearls are sometimes given a faux natural surface to fool prospective buyers.

• Hold the pearls under a bright light, either indoors or outdoors. Study them for variations in colour and iridescence – if the pearls are identical in shape and colour they are fake.

• Use a magnifying glass to look for irregularities such as bumps or pits over the surface and carefully inspect the drill hole. If you can see layers, they are probably the real deal.

• Go for quality. Real pearls are heavier than fake, tend to be knotted between each pearl and have sterling-silver catches with safety chains.

Caring for Fine Jewellery

Jewellery that contains precious gemstones such as diamonds should be stored individually because even the hardest stones can chip. Individual cloth pouches may be purchased from most jewellery stores and will prevent stones from accidentally scuffing one another in your jewellery box. Antique diamonds must be cleaned by a professional as both stones and settings may be delicate and need expert attention. For cleaning other gemstones the following tools are recommended:

• Shallow dish – never clean in a sink as an unstable plug could lead to disaster! Presoak your jewellery here.

• Soft bristle toothbrush to remove dirt from your jewellery with no abrasion.

• Mild detergent.

• Lint-free cloth – those used for cleaning glasses are perfect.

Step 1: Remove any fibres affixed to the prongs of settings with tweezers.
Step 2: Place the piece in a mild solution of detergent and water then scrub lightly with the toothbrush, changing angles as you go.
Step 3: Rinse carefully in fresh water and finally, dry and buff with a soft cloth.

LEFT An ornate costume "Parrot" bracelet by Canadian jeweller Alan Anderson. Anderson specializes in making new pieces with unusual vintage stones from his collection.

Caring for Pearls

Pearls are delicate and prone to damage from pollution; they are also susceptible to staining from cosmetics, perfume and hairspray so make them the last thing you put on before you go out. They should never be cleaned with any kind of solvent or abrasive but merely wiped with a soft, lint-free cloth. Keep away from the beach or pool when wearing pearls – the silk string on which they are usually strung deteriorates quickly when wet and pearls should never be exposed to chlorinated water or sunscreen. Wipe with a lint-free cloth after wear because the more that pearls come into contact with the skin, the quicker they lose their lustre. Keep out of the sunlight and avoid cooking when wearing pearls – they are organic and can become dehydrated and damaged when exposed to too much heat.

Bakelite or Fakelite?

An enormous amount of fake Bakelite (or Fakelite) is on the market at the moment, much of it produced in India. Watch out for large multicoloured polka-dot bangles, figurative rings with motifs such as Scottie dogs and obviously "antiqued" hinges. Martha Sleeper pieces are being reproduced in this way – if an item looks cheap with no obvious signs of wear, avoid it, as all her work is old and extremely rare. To test for the real thing, give a brisk rub with your thumb on a piece of Bakelite and then quickly smell it – it should have a resinous or camphor-like odour. Or, if at home with a flea-market find, place under hot running water for 30 seconds and, again, sniff it to detect the smell of phenol. If the phenol aroma swiftly disappears to leave a plastic smell, it's Fakelite.

- With so much fake Bakelite about, it's best to visit a reputable dealer rather than to buy from the Internet – leave that to the experts.

- No Bakelite is produced today. Dealers may refer to "new Bakelite" but it is, in fact, polymer.

- There is no such thing as "white" Bakelite; it darkens and turns slightly yellow with age.

- Study the fastening and hinges and how they have been attached to the piece. Old Bakelite pieces have small holes drilled into them with pins, rivets or screws for fixings – they will not be glued.

Caring for Bakelite

Bakelite is sensitive to sunlight, which causes it to discolour or fade, so keep it out of direct light and store by wrapping in a soft cloth. It does not respond well to changes in temperature and can occasionally craze or crack in contact with a radiator or air-conditioner, or when stored in plastic. Wash by hand with soapy water, dry with a towel and then apply a polish such as Turtle Wax or Simichrome to buff and remove minor scuffmarks.

Buying Online

Be canny if you decide to buy online – as recommended earlier, it is best to do this only if you are a very experienced collector. If a seller produces a number of pieces of vintage jewellery from one well-known designer such as Schiaparelli, the authenticity could well be dubious – it's highly unlikely that anyone would dispose of a whole collection all at once. It's also easy to research the seller by looking carefully at their feedback. If it's a private sale, it's advisable not to buy – you will have no idea of their reputation. Read the details in the item listings carefully because if the piece you buy has been misrepresented, then you may be able to get your money back.

Be sure to take the delivery charges into consideration and check that your item is insured if it's to be shipped – also be aware that you may incur quite hefty import charges if you purchase from overseas. If you buy from anyone other than through eBay you will not be covered should anything go wrong; never pay for any item using an instant cash wire transfer service – it can be extremely unsafe with a dealer you do not know. If you buy through eBay using Paypal, the seller will never be given any bank or credit card details about you apart from your address, and if you have PayPal Buyer Protection, your purchase can be covered up to $1,000.

ABOVE A citrine ring and drop earring set, circa 1920s. Buying a vintage piece in its original box will help authenticate its provenance and therefore its value.

Museums and Collections

UNITED KINGDOM

Brighton Museum & Art Gallery
Royal Pavilion Gardens
Brighton
East Sussex BN1 1EE
Tel: 03000 290900
www.brighton-hove-rpml.org.uk/
museums/brightonmuseum
A good collection of Art Nouveau
jewellery, including pieces from
several countries.

British Museum
Great Russell Street
London WC1B 3DG
Tel: 020 7323 8000
www.britishmuseum.org
The collection includes jewellery
from about 5000 BC to the present
day. Much of it is on public
display, while more is accessible
via the museum's online
collection.

**Cheltenham Art Gallery &
Museum**
Clarence Street
Cheltenham GL50 3JT
Tel: 01242 237431
www.cheltenhammuseum.org.uk
Outstanding permanent
collection including Arts and
Crafts silver and jewellery by
Charles Ashbee's Guild of
Handicraft.

The Fashion Museum
Assembly Rooms
Bennett Street
Bath BA1 2QH
Tel: 01225 477789
www.museumofcostume.co.uk
Small collection of costume
jewellery dating from the
eighteenth to the twenty-first
century. Includes hatpins,
buckles, brooches, necklaces,
earrings, bracelets and tiaras.
Although the costume jewellery
is not on display in the museum,
an active study facility enables
access to the collection.

Museum of London
150 London Wall
London EC2Y 5HN
Tel: 020 7001 9844
www.museumoflondon.org.uk
This fine jewellery collection
includes groups assembled
by such notable collectors as
Dame Joan Evans, Baroness
D'Erlanger, Lady Cory and Queen
Mary. Includes the Cheapside
hoard – the greatest collection of
Elizabeth and Jacobean jewellery
in the world.

**Museum of the Jewellery
Quarter**
75–79 Vyse Street
Hockley
Birmingham B18 6HA
Tel: 0121 554 3598
www.bmag.org.uk/museum-of-
the-jewellery-quarter
The story of the Jewellery
Quarter and Birmingham's
renowned jewellery and metal-
making heritage. The Earth's
Riches gallery showcases pieces
made from materials from the
natural world, including whale
tooth, coral, diamonds
and platinum.

Tower of London
London EC3N 4AB
Tel: 0844 482 7777
www.hrp.org.uk/toweroflondon
Be dazzled by the 23,578 gems
that make up the Crown Jewels,
including the world's most
famous diamonds.

The Ulster Museum
Botanic Gardens
Belfast BT9 5AB
Tel: 0845 608 0000
www.nmni.com
Particularly strong in eighteenth-
century paste, nineteenth-
century jewellery and Art
Nouveau pieces. Includes the
most complete collection of
nineteenth-century Irish jewellery
in existence; also pre-historic and
early medieval Irish jewellery.

Victoria and Albert Museum
Cromwell Road
London SW7 2RL
Tel: 020 7942 2000
www.vam.ac.uk
The William and Judith Bollinger
Jewellery Gallery displays 3,500
jewels from the V&A's jewellery
collection, one of the finest and
most comprehensive in the world.

Whitby Museum
Pannett Park
Whitby
North Yorkshire YO21 1RE
Tel: 01947 602908
www.whitbymuseum.org.uk
One of the best collections of jet
artefacts in the world with over
500 examples.

UNITED STATES

**American Museum
of Natural History**
Central Park West at 79th Street
New York NY 10024-5192
Tel: 212 769 5100
www.amnh.org
Twenty-five dazzling diamonds
are on display in the Morgan
Memorial Hall of Gems.

Brooklyn Museum
200 Eastern Parkway
Brooklyn
New York NY 11238-6052
Tel: 718 638 5000
www.brooklynmuseum.org
One of America's largest
museums with collections that
include jewellery from Ancient
Egypt to the present day.

**Luce Foundation Center
for American Art**
Smithsonian American Art Museum
8th and F Streets, N.W.
Washington DC 20004
Tel: 202 633 1000
www.exhibitfiles.org/the_luce_
foundation_center_for_american_
art
A storage and study centre, with
public space, that holds a large
collection of antique and more
contemporary jewellery.

AUSTRALIA

The National Opal Collection
Level 1
119 Swanston Street
Melbourne VIC 3000
Tel: 613 9662 3524
www.nationalopal.com
Retail showroom and museum
that displays a huge variety of
Australia's national gemstone
and explains how they were
formed and mined.

BELGIUM

The Diamond Museum
Koningin Astridplein 19
2018 Antwerpen
Belgium.
Tel: 32 3 202 48 90
www.provant.be/vrije_tijd/cultuur/
musea/diamantmuseum
Antwerp is the diamond centre of
the world. This museum covers
every aspect of diamonds,
including a collection of diamond
jewellery from the sixteenth
century to the present day.

DENMARK

**The National Museum of
Denmark (Nationalmuseet)**
Frederiksholms Kanal 12
DK 1220 Copenhagen K
Tel: (45) 3313 4411
www.natmus.dk
Danish pre-historic and Viking
jewellery; some Amager and
North African traditional jewellery.

FINLAND

The National Museum of Finland
Mannerheimintie 34
00100 Helsinki
Tel: (358) 40 1286469
www.nba.fi/en/nationalmuseum
Finno-Ugric traditional jewellery
from Finland, Estonia and Russia.

FRANCE

Musée des Arts Décoratifs
107 rue de Rivoli
75001 Paris
Tel: 00 331 4455 5750
www.lesartsdecoratifs.fr
Around 1,200 jewels are
exhibited in the Galerie des
Bijoux.

Musée d'Orsay
5 Quai Anatole
75007 Paris
Tel: 00 331 4049 4814
www.musee-orsay.fr
Fine collection of jewellery and
goldsmiths' work from the 1860s.

Musée du Louvre
34–36 Quai du Louvre
75001 Paris
Tel: 00 33 (0) 1 4020 5317
www.louvre.fr
Collection of jewellery ranging
from ancient to mid-nineteenth
century; includes the magnificent
French Crown jewels display in
Galerie d'Apollon.

**Musée Lalique (Musée
de France)**
40 rue du Hochberg
67290 Wingen-sur-Moder
Tel: 00 33 388 890814
www.musee-lalique.com
The only museum in France
dedicated to the work of Art
Nouveau master jeweller and
glass worker, René Lalique.

GERMANY
Fabergé Museum GmbH
Sophie Strasse 30
76530 Baden-Baden
Tel: 49 (0) 7221 970890
www.fabergemuseum.de
Dedicated solely to the life and
work of Carl Fabergé, including
exquisite jewellery.

Schmuckmuseum Pforzheim
Jahnstrasse 42
75172 Pforzheim
Tel: 00 49 7231 392126
www.schmuckmuseum.de
One of the few dedicated
jewellery museums in the world.
A permanent exhibition from
Antiquity to the present day,
plus a rolling schedule of
temporary exhibitions.

GREECE
**The Ilias Lalaounis
Jewellery Museum**
Kallisperi 12 and Karyatidon Street
Acropolis 11742
Athens
Tel: 30 210 8217717
www.lalaounis-jewelrymuseum.gr
The only museum worldwide
dedicated to contemporary
jewellery with over 4,000 pieces
and micro sculptures.

National Archaeological Museum
44 Patission St
Athens
Tel (30) 210 8217717
www.namuseum.gr
Classical jewellery including the
treasure from Mycenae.

HUNGARY
Museum of Applied Arts
H-1091 Budapest
Ullol ut 33–37
Tel: 36 1 456 5107
www.imm.hu
Includes a number of outstanding
Art Nouveau jewels, such as
works by Rene Lalique and
Oszkár Tarján (Huber).

ITALY
Museo degli Argenti
Palazzo Pitti 1
50125 Florence
Tel: 055 238 8709
www.uffizi.firenze.it/musei/argenti
Over 500 pieces from the
seventeenth century to the
present day.

NETHERLANDS
Galerie Marzee
Lage Markt 3
6511 VK Nijmegen
Tel: (31) 243229670
www.marzee.nl
The largest gallery for modern
jewellery in the world: hosts four
or five exhibitions at any time with
new openings every two months.

POLAND
The Amber Museum
Targ Weglowy, 26
Gdansk
Tel: (48) 58 301 47 33
www.mhmg.gda.pl
Museum dedicated to amber,
including the achievements of
contemporary amber artists.

Stores and Boutiques
UNITED KINGDOM
Blackout II
51 Endell Street
Covent Garden
London WC2H 9AJ
Tel: 020 7240 5006
www.blackout2.com
Vintage costume jewellery.

Cenci
4 Nettlefold Place
London SE27 OJW
Tel: 020 8766 8564
www.cenci.co.uk
Vintage fashion, accessories
and jewellery from the
1930s onwards.

Electrum Gallery
21 South Molton Street
London W1K 5QZ
Tel: 020 7629 6325
www.electrumgallery.co.uk
For unique contemporary
jewellery from Tone Vigelund,
Wendy Ramshaw, Gerda
Flöckinger, and more.

Linda Bee
Grays Antique Market
58 Davies Street and
1–7 Davies Mews
London W1K 5AB
Tel: 020 7629 5921
www.graysantiques.com
Long-established dealer in
London's Grays Antiques Market.

Obsidian, Harry Fane
Tel: 020 7930 8606
www.harryfane.com
A world authority on vintage
Cartier and Verdura.

Palette London
21 Canonbury Lane
London N1 2AS
Tel: 020 7 288 7428
www.palette-london.com
Eclectic mix of quirky vintage
jewellery from the 1920s to
the 1990s. There is also a
finder service.

Rellik
8 Golborne Road
London W10 5NW
Tel: 020 8962 0089
www.relliklondon.co.uk
Clothing and accessories from
the 1920s to mid-1980s.

Rokit
42 Shelton Street
London WC2H 9HZ
Tel: 020 7836 6547
www.rokit.co.uk
Vintage and retro clothing
and jewellery from the 1920s
to the 1980s.

Tadema Gallery
10 Charlton Place
London N1 8AJ
Tel: 020 7359 1055
www.tademagallery.com
Specialists in late nineteenth and
early twentieth-century jewellery:
Art Nouveau, Jugendstil,
Skonvirke, British Arts and Crafts,
Egyptian Revival, Art Deco and
Mid-Century jewellery.

Van den Bosch
123 Grays Antique Market
58 Davies Streeet
London W1K 5LP
Tel: 020 7629 1900
www.vandenbosch.co.uk
Jewellery from the Arts and
Crafts, Art Nouveau, Jugendstil
and Skonvirke movements.

UNITED STATES
Annie Cream Cheese
of Las Vegas
3327 Las Vegas Boulevard South
Las Vegas NV 89109
Tel: 702 452 9600
www.anniecreamcheese.com
High-end designer vintage
clothing; also stocks a large
selection of vintage jewellery.

Decades Two
8214 Melrose Ave
Los Angeles CA 90046
Tel: 323 655 1960
www.decadestwo.com
Vintage couture boutique with
a carefully edited selection of
designs from the 1930s to the
1990s that often appear on
the red carpet during awards
seasons.

CANADA
Deluxe Junk Company
310 Cordova Street West
Vancouver
British Columbia V6B 1E8
Tel: 604 685 4871
www.deluxejunk.com
Vancouver's oldest vintage
clothing and accessories store.

Divine Decadence Originals
128 Cumberland Street
Upper Floor
Toronto
Ontario M5R 1A6
Tel: 416 324 9759
www.divinedecadenceoriginals.
com
Vintage clothing and jewellery.

AUSTRALIA
Vintage Clothing Shop
7/80 Castlereagh Street
Sydney 2000
Tel: 612 9238 0090
Unusual and eclectic selection of
quality original vintage clothing
and jewellery.

Antique Markets
Most cities have weekly, or even
daily, antique or flea markets
where time and patience may be
rewarded with some lucky finds.

UNITED KINGDOM
Bermondsey Market
Bermondsey Square
Tower Bridge Road, London
http://bermondseysquare.co.uk/
antiques.html
Every Friday 4am–1pm.
This historical market needs an
early start, but it's worth the effort

Portobello Road Market
Portobello Road, London
www.portobello road.co.uk
Market every Saturday, shops are
open six days a week.
Europe's largest market with
plenty of vintage jewellery finds.

UNITED STATES
Antiques Garage
112 W 25th between 6th
and 7th Aves
New York, NY 10001
Tel: 212 243 5343
www.hellskitchenfleamarket.com
Saturday and Sunday, 9am–5pm.
More than 100 vendors, located
in a Manhattan parking garage.

Hell's Kitchen Flea Market
6th Ave
New York, NY 10001
Tel: 212 243 5343
www.hellskitchenfleamarket.com
Every Sunday 9am–6pm.
Small second hand market that
gets busy quickly, so arrive early.

FRANCE
Clignancourt Market
79 Boulevard Ornano
75018 Paris
Tel: 33 1 4223 3954
www.marchesauxpuces.fr
Mon–Sat, 9am–6pm.
A grouping of 2,000–3,000 stalls
on the northern fringe of the city.

Lille Flea Market
www.lilletourism.com
First week of September.
For two days a year the streets
of Lille are transformed into a
bargain hunters dream, with
100 km (62 miles) of stalls and
10,000 exhibitors.

Charity/Thrift Stores
Keep an eye on your local
charity or thrift stores for lucky
finds; visit their websites to
discover your local stores.

UNITED KINGDOM
Barnardo's
www.barnardos.org.uk

British Heart Foundation
www.bhf.org.uk

British Red Cross
www.redcross.org.uk

Cancer Research UK
www.cancerresearchuk.org

Marie Curie
www.mariecurie.org.uk

Oxfam
www.oxfam.org.uk

Save the Children
www.savethechildren.org.uk

Sue Ryder
www.sueryder.org

UNITED STATES
Arc Thrift Stores
www.arcthrift.com

Goodwill Industries
International
www.goodwill.org

Salvation Army
www.salvationarmyusa.org

CANADA
Goodwill Industries
International
www.goodwill.on.ca

AUSTRALIA
Brotherhood of St Laurence
www.bsl.org.au

Salvation Army
salvos.org.au

Society of Saint Vincent de Paul
www.vinnies.org.au

Online Stores
www.affordablevintagejewelry.com
www.agedandopulentjewelry.com
www.anniesherman.com
www.bagladyemporium.com
www.bejewelledvintage.co.uk
www.chicagosilver.com
www.decogirl.co.uk
www.druckerantiques.com
www.heirloomjewellery.com
www.heritagejewellery.co.uk
www.jacksonjewels.com
www.laurelleantiquejewellery.co.uk
www.magpievintage.co.uk
www.modernity.se
www.morninggloryjewelry.com
www.pastperfectvintage.com
www.penelopespearls.com
www.rubylane.com
www.scandinaviansilver.co.uk
www.thejewelrystylist.com
http://v4vintage.com
www.vintagecostumejewels.com
www.vintagejewelryonline.com
www.wartski.com

Auction Houses
UNITED KINGDON
Bonhams
101 New Bond Street
London W1S 1SR
Tel: 020 7447 7447
and
13 Montpelier Street
London SW7 1HH
Tel: 020 7393 3900
www.bonhams.com

Christie's
8 King Street
St James's
London SW1Y 6QT
Tel: 020 7839 9060
and
85 Old Brompton Road
London SW7 3LD
Tel: 020 7930 6074
www.christies.com

Sotheby's
Tel: 020 7293 5000
www.sothebys.com

UNITED STATES
Bonhams
220 San Bruno Avenue
San Francisco CA 94103
Tel: 415 861 7500
and
7601 Sunset Boulevard
Los Angeles CA 90046
Tel: 323 850 7500
and
580 Madison Avenue
New York NY 10022
Tel: 212 644 9009
www.bonhams.com

Christie's
1230 Avenue of the Americas
New York NY 10020
Tel: 212 636 2000
www.christies.com

Sotheby's
Tel: 212 606 7000
www.sothebys.com

CANADA
Bonhams
20 Hazelton
Toronto ON M5R 2E2
Tel: 416 513 1273
www.bonhams.com

AUSTRALIA
Bonhams
76 Paddington Street
Paddington
NSW 2021
Tel: 612 8412 2222
www.bonhams.com

Contributors

Many thanks to the online shops below for their archive resources, information and advice. Please see individual listings for vintage jewellery-buying information.

Affordable Vintage Jewelry
www.affordablevintagejewelry.com
Contact: Polly Curtiss
Tel: (001) 860 417 3262
Vintage, antique and estate jewellery with an emphasis on vintage sterling silver.

Aged and Opulent Jewelry
www.agedandopulentjewelry.com
Specializes in high-end vintage costume jewellery.

Bag Lady Emporium.com
www.bagladyemporium.com
Contact: Marion Spitzley
bagladyemporium@gmail.com
Bakelite and plastic jewellery, as well as signed and unsigned.

Butterfly Blue
www.rubylane.com/shop/
butterflyblue
Contact: Patricia Howard
Tel: (001) 604 948 8686

Chicago Silver
www.chicagosilver.com
American Arts and Crafts, focusing on the Kalo Shop.

Decogirl
www.decogirl.co.uk
Contact: Wanda Ingham
decogirl@sky.com
Tel: (44) 07525 203928
Specializing in Bakelite and plastics, especially Lea Stein.

Drucker Antiques
www.druckerantiques.com
Contact: William Drucker
bill@druckerantiques.com
For Georg Jensen.

Enchantiques
www.etsy.com/shop/
enchantiques
For vintage 1950s and 1960s, including Eisenberg Originals.

Green's
www.rubylane.com/shop/greens
Contact: Susie Green
Tel: (44) 020 7435 4085

The Jewelry Stylist
www.thejewelrystylist.com
Contact: Melinda Lewis, stylist at thejewelrystylist.com
Tel: (001) 707 751 1665
Costume jewellery, including parures and individual pieces by Haskell, Schreiner, Trifari, Schiaparelli, YSL and Chanel.

Lets Get Vintage
www.letsgetvintage.com

Little Shiny Objects
www.rubylane.com/shop/
littleshinyobjects
Contact: Marcy Drexler
Tel: (917) 488 7555

Melange-Art
www.rubylane.com/shops/
melange-art
Linda Sweeney
Tel: (001) 520 403 4794

Modernity
www.modernity.se
info@modernity.se
Tel: (46) 8 20 80 25
For Scandinavian Modern, such as pieces by Torun Bülow-Hübe.

Morning Glory Antiques and Jewelry
www.morninggloryjewelry.com
Costume jewellery, including Juliana, Haskell, Trifari, Swarovski, Coro, Eisenberg and Weiss, as well as plastic.

Past Perfect Vintage
www.pastperfectvintage.com
Contact: montyholly@insightbb.com
montyholly@insightbb.com
Tel: (001) 502 718 9190

Penelope's Pearls Vintage and Antique Jewelry
www.penelopespearls.com
Contact: Nancy Bohm
Tel: (44) 519 773 3587

Two Silly Magpies
www.rubylane.com/shops/
twosillymagpies
Contact: Patti Williamson

Glossary of Jewellery Terms

A jour: Opening in a gemstone setting that allows light to pass through the stone from both sides.

Aguette: Gemstone, often a diamond, cut in a narrow, rectangular shape. Small diamonds cut in this way are often used as accents.

Aigrette: Very popular in the early twentieth century, this hair ornament was often decorated with feathers or glitter.

Ajoure: Design with holes punched, cut or drilled into a piece of metal rather than wires, which have been bent or formed into the design, as with filigree.

Alloy: Metallurgical term for a mixture of two or more metals. In jewellery, most metals are alloyed together, either to alter the colour of the metal or to give it greater strength.

Amulet: Object or a talisman to protect against danger and the unknown.

Anodizing: Technique used to dye and/or modify the surface of a metal (usually titanium) using electrolysis.

Art Deco: Popular during the early twentieth century from the 1910s, the style originated in France and is characterized by geometric designs and angles.

Art Nouveau: Designs from the late nineteenth and early twentieth century which made their way into jewellery making, often characterized by curved, flowing, asymmetrical lines. Many designs feature leaves, flowers, insects and *femme fatales*.

Aurora borealis: Name for a particular type of rhinestone with an iridescent finish; a process created by Swarovski and Christian Dior in 1955.

Baguette: Small, rectangular-shaped stones with facets.

Bakelite: Synthetic resin invented in 1909. Made from phenol and formaldehyde, it is characterized by its hardness and was used extensively in jewellery of the 1960s.

Bar brooch or pin: Long, narrow brooch or pin often set with gemstones.

Baroque pearl: Sometimes also referred to as a "potato pearl", this is an irregularly shaped pearl or stone and favoured by Miriam Haskell.

Basse-taille: Translucent enamelling applied over an engraved metal surface; popular with mid twentieth-century Scandinavian silversmiths.

Bevel cut: Where the surface has been cut at an angle of less than 90 degrees.

Bezel: A band with a groove or flange. A setting that involves a metal band (bezel) that encircles the gemstone and extends slightly above it and holds the gem in place.

Brilliant cut: The most popular cut shape for diamonds, its shape resembles a cone and is intended to maximize light return through the top of the stone.

Briolette: A drop-shaped stone with triangular or diamond-shaped facets all the way around.

Butterfly wing jewellery: Jewellery made from real butterfly wings. Often a picture depicted by reverse painting, the whole thing is then encased in plastic or glass.

Cable chain: Style of chain whose links are round and uniform in size.

Cabochon: Gemstone cut with a rounded, domed surface, with no facets. Usually round or oval, but can be other shapes. Denser semiprecious stones such as turquoise or tiger's-eye are mainly given the cabochon cut as they do not need as much light to penetrate their beauty.

Cameo: Carving in which the surrounding surface of a design is cut away to leave the design in relief.

Cannetille: Wire filigree braided to form a cone-shaped scroll or spiral. Used as a gem setting framework.

Carat: Unit of weight used to describe diamonds and other precious gems. The metric carat of 200 milligrams was adopted by the US in the early 1900s and is now universally used. Also known as karat and used as a measure of purity for gold. See also **Karat**.

Cartouche: Decoration characterized by swirls and scrollwork in a symmetrical design.

Catalin: Early form of phenol plastic material sometimes referred to as Bakelite, although the composition is a little different.

Chamlevé: An enamelling technique where grooves are cut into the metal and filled with enamel.

Channel setting: Two strips of metal (gold, platinum or silver) are used to hold gemstones in place at the sides, with no metal between the stones. It is better than a prong setting for small stones.

Chaton setting: This setting holds a stone in place through a series of metal claws around a metal ring; also referred to as a coronet or arcade setting.

Chatoyancy: Strip of light reflected onto the surface of a stone that glints back and forth, resembling a cat's eye.

Claw setting: Often employed so that the back of the stone can be open to allow more light to pass through, this is a setting in which the stone is held in place by a number of metal prongs (claws).

Clip-back/Clip-on: Earrings designed for non-pierced ears.

Cliquet: Also known as a jabot pin, or *sûreté*, this is a fastening device that uses a pin-and-snap closure.

Cloisonne: Multistep process whereby filigree is inlaid with enamel to produce a glassy sheen and a wide variety of colours.

Collier de chien: Wide, ornamented, jewelled necklace worn tightly round a woman's throat, also known as a "dog collar".

Confetti Lucite: Form of plastic Lucite which is transparent with chips or glitter encased inside.

Crown: Top half of a gemstone.

Cushion: This can be a type of diamond cut incorporating both a round and square shape. Also refers to a style of signet ring stamping.

Damascene: Process of applying gold or silver onto iron or steel to produce intricate patterns. Damascene jewellery often comes from Spain or Japan.

Decoration etched: Very faintly carved surface decoration.

Demantoid garnet: Sub-variety of andradite; the rarest and most expensive of garnets, the colour ranges from dark- to yellowish-green.

Diadem: Ornamented band, often with gemstones, worn around the brow. More recent examples were made in Art Nouveau style.

Diamanté (rhinestone): A diamond substitute made from rock crystal, glass or acrylic.

Duette: Combination two-part pin on one pin back, made famous by Coro.

Electroplating: Method of finishing a metal in which an electric current puts a layer of metal on another alloy.

Emerald cut: Often but not always an emerald, this is a stepped, normally rectangular gemstone cut with cropped corners.

En esclavage: Bracelet or necklace containing similar metal plaques connected by rows of swagged chain ("enslaved").

Enamel: Glass-like decorative surface produced by fusing coloured powdered glass "paste" to metal (usually bronze, copper or gold).

Engrave: Gouging out a design in metal with engraver's tools, or embellishing metal or other material with patterns using a stamping tool or drill.

Facet: The polished face of a gemstone.

Faceted: Small, flat-cut surfaces that make a sparkling effect on transparent stones. Diamonds, rubies and sapphires are nearly always faceted (the opposite of cabochon).

Fakelite: Modern, mass-produced product; neither true Bakelite nor vintage (also known as French Bakelite).

Ferronière: Headdress featuring a thin metal band adorned with a single large gemstone.

Festoon: Design motif consisting of a garland or string of flowers, ribbons or leaves.

Filigree: Technique used to produce delicate, intricate patterns in gold or silver wire twisted into patterns. Often used for metal beads and clasps.

Fox tail chain: A type of woven chain made from many individual, interlinked links.

French backs: An earring back for non-pierced ears where the earring is tightened against the earlobes by means of a screw. Also referred to as a screwback earring.

Fruit Salad jewellery: Also known as "tutti frutti" and made of glass or plastic stones in the shape of fruits or leaves.

Garland style: Popular in the early twentieth century and made possible by the widespread use of platinum. Characterized by lightness and delicacy that employed motifs such as garlands, ribbon bows, swags and tassels.

Girandole: Chandelier-like brooch or earrings with three pear-shaped pendants hanging from a larger central setting.

Givre stones: Stones made of transparent glass fused around a translucent core to give a frosted appearance.

Gold filled: Looking like carat gold and often referred to as rolled gold, gold-filled pieces must be at least one twentieth by weight in gold to be classified as such.

Gold-plated: Finish where a very thin layer of gold is applied to the surface of a piece, usually by electroplating; often marked GEP, gold plated or gold electroplate.

Grain: Unit sometimes used to measure pearls – a metric or pearl grain is equal to 50 milligrams or a quarter of a carat.

Grooved: Routed out in a line.

Guilloché: Machine-turning technique for engraving a repetitive decorative pattern onto a metal surface.

Guilloché enamel: Translucent enamel is applied to metal, which has detailed engraving on it.

Habillé: Refers to the image in a cameo of a woman wearing some form of gem-set jewellery.

Hallmark: Official stamped mark applied to metal items by the Assay Offices of Britain as a guarantee of authenticity and to indicate metal content.

Hammered finish: Indented hammer marks on a metal's surface.

Inclusion: Particle of solid, liquid or gaseous foreign matter contained within a stone.

Inlaid: Technique where a space is routed out of metal and a contrasting material fitted into that space. Bakelite polka-dot bracelets are an excellent example.

Intaglio: Opposite of cameo, this is a carved gem from which the design is engraved or carved into the object.

Iridescence: Optical phenomenon in which the hue on the surface of the stone changes according to the angle from which the surface is viewed.

Jabot pin: Tiepin accented with jewels, popular in the early twentieth century.

Jarretière: Type of metal bracelet with a strap and buckle on one end and a mordant at the other.

Jelly Belly pin: Style of figural brooch made famous by Trifari and Coro with a clear lucite cabochon that forms the "belly" of the piece.

Juliana: Style of jewellery, not a maker, these pieces were designed by the DeLizza and Elster factory and are highly collectable. The jewellery itself is never marked, only with paper hanging tags.

Karat (or carat): Usually abbreviated to the letter "K", karat refers to the purity of gold: 24K is 100 per cent pure gold, 18K is 18 parts gold with six parts other alloyed metals.

Lariat: Long necklace with open ends (no clasp), kept in place by knotting or looping the ends.

Lavaliere: Pendant with a dangling stone below it.

Liberty style: A style associated with the famous London store epitomizing the Art Nouveau look of the early twentieth century.

Limoges: French technique for enamelling and firing to create a pictorial image, usually a portrait, to be used as a brooch.

Lobster claw: Clasp resembling a lobster's claw with a spring mechanism that can be opened to attach to the other end of the chain.

Loupe: Magnifying glass used by jewellers to see the inclusions and imperfections inside gemstones with a 10-times magnification.

Lucite: Thermoplastic acrylic resin (strong plastic) patented by the DuPont company in 1941; lucite has a specific gravity of 1.19 and is clear. Due to its transparent nature it was easily coloured or more interestingly mixed with glitter or other small pieces of material, which is known as "Confetti Lucite".

Maltese cross: Cross with four arms of equal length; the width of each arm widens, the further it gets from the centre.

Manchette: Wide bracelet tapering into the shape of a shirtsleeve.

Marquise cut: Elongated, faceted oval cut tapering to a point. Similar to a navette cut (see below), but slightly more rounded.

Matinée length: Single-strand necklace 56–58 cm (22–23 in) long.

Metal inlay: Imbedding or insertion of sheet metal or wire into an indentation or groove in the surface of a finished piece of metal.

Millegrain setting: Where a gemstone is secured with tiny beads that are fashioned from metal.

Mirror finish: Highly reflective surface with no visible abrasion pattern. Created with rouge, muslin or a flannel buffing wheel.

Mohs scale: Comparison chart developed in the early part of the 1800s. It tells us how hard minerals are in comparison to others – useful when buying or storing gemstones.

Mother-of-pearl: Hard, smooth, pearlized inside linings of abalone and other shellfish, scraped off and used as an inlay.

Navette: Oval stone which is pointed at both ends.

Navette cut: Oblong, tapered slender cut similar to a Marquise, although more slender.

Négligée: Necklace pendant with two unevenly suspended drops.

Nickel silver: Also referred to as "German silver", this alloy contains no actual silver but mainly copper, with approximately 20 per cent nickel and 20 per cent zinc.

Opalescence: Named after the appearance of opals, a material appears yellowish-red in transmitted light and blue in scattered light.

Open-backed: Use of a setting for a stone where the stone is set in a metal frame with an open back, which allows more light to pass through.

Opera length: Single-strand necklace 76–89 cm (30–35 in) in length; it hangs to the breastbone.

Ormolu: Refers to gilded bronze or brass mounts.

Pampille: Graduated row of articulating set gemstones that taper to a point.

Parure: Matching set of jewellery; usually a brooch, necklace, earrings and a bracelet, but can be larger. Part of a parure is called a demi- or semi-parure.

Paste: Brilliant-cut glass stone made to resemble a genuine gemstone.

Paste diamantés: Beautifully crafted, PD stones are made from high-quality cut crystals that can be open or foil-backed.

Patina: Chemical film formed on the surface of metal through wear, corrosion or oxidization; often deliberately added by metalworkers.

Pavé: The process of setting stones, where a number of small stones are set as closely together as possible. Better pieces employ a claw setting.

Pavé cut: Pinpoint gemstones or diamonds set close together to create a field of colour.

Pavilion: Lower half of a gemstone.

Pendeloque: Pear-shaped gemstone cut, or a pear-shaped drop earring suspended from a circular or bow setting.

Piqué: Gold or silver inlay design pattern (pricked). Also a carbon diamond inclusion.

Plique-à-jour: Translucent enamelling technique with the look of stained glass.

Princess length: Single-strand necklace, which is 45 cm (18 in) long.

Prong: Setting with a series of metal prongs that grip around the side of stones. Better rhinestone jewellery is prong set rather than glued.

Repoussé: French for "to push back", repoussé is a technique for creating a relief design by pressing or hammering the inside or back of a metal surface.

Reticulation: Giving a metal surface a rough or wrinkled texture with a naturally formed appearance. Also known as Samorodok, this process was popularized by Russian artists such as Fabergé.

Rhinestones: Cut-glass stones; usually small and circular, often foil-backed to increase their reflectivity and sparkle. Rhinestones may be used as imitations of diamonds.

Rivière: Necklace of ascending graduated gemstones or diamonds.

Rondelle: Usually comprizes two circular discs, often decorated with rhinestones on their outer edges – which Chanel uses as decorative spacers in more elaborate necklaces.

Rose cut: This standard rose cut for diamonds, also known as the Dutch rose cut, has 24 triangular facets: six star facets meet at a point at the top and 18 cross facets.

Rose montee: A rhinestone that comes pre-mounted in a metal cup with holes in it.

Rose recoupée: Style of cutting a diamond (or other transparent gemstone) in the basic rose-cut fashion but with a 12-sided base and 36 facets cut in two horizontal rows.

Sautoir: Long necklace of beads or pearls, often ending in a tassel, and very popular in the 1920s.

Sawing: Technique developed in the early twentieth century for dividing a rough diamond before bruting (shaping) and faceting.

Schiller: Flecks in the iridescent colour display found in labradorite and moonstone.

Scroll piece: Component used in the manufacture of earrings for pierced ears, it holds the earring onto the ear by attaching to the pin. Also known as "butterfly".

Seed pearl: Very small round pearl.

Shank: Portion of a ring that encircles a finger.

Shot ball: Using tiny shot balls fused to the metal's surface to create a pattern or design and add texture.

Snake link chain: The links actually made of wavy metal plates joined together to form a tube.

Solder: Fusible metal alloy (gold solder: gold mixed with lower melting metals) with a melting point below 450°C (840°F), which is melted to join two metallic surfaces.

Step cut: Term used for stones which are rectangular and whose facets are parallel to the edge of the stone in a "stepped" effect and with a flat top.

Sterling silver: Alloy that is 925 parts pure silver and 75 parts copper.

Sûreté: Also known as a cliquet or jabot pin, this is a fastening device that uses a pin-and-snap closure.

Taille d'epargne: Enamelling technique where outlines or shallow channels are engraved into the metal, then filled with opaque black, blue or red enamel.

Tiara: Of Persian origin, a decorative, flowered or jewelled headband worn in the front of the hair for special occasions.

Tiffany mounting: Solitaire mounting with a four- or six-prong head to hold the diamond. The shank is usually simple and narrow.

Torsade: Necklace comprizing many strands twisted together instead of left to hang loosely.

Translucent: Allowing light to pass through, but the light is scattered. Translucent stones include moonstones, opals and carnelian.

Transparent: Permitting light to pass through without scattering so that it is possible to see right through. Transparent stones include diamond, sapphire, emerald and ruby.

Trombone clasp: Mostly used on a brooch or pin, this is a metal "stopper" that is pulled out along the back of the pin to release a prong.

Tutti Frutti: *See* **Fruit Salad jewellery**.

Verdigris: Green patina that can develop over time on costume or fine jewellery. Its presence means there is metal damage underneath.

Vermeil: Sterling silver with a layer of gold applied on top; the gold must be at least 10 carat.

Picture Credits

The publishers would like to thank the following sources for their kind permission to reproduce the pictures in this book.

Key: t=Top, b=Bottom, c=Centre, l=Left and r=Right

Alamy: Antiques & Collectables: 30b, 31c

Alinari Picture Library: Fratelli Alinari Museum Collections-Nunes Vais Archives, Florence: 12

Bag Lady Emporium: Courtesy Marion Spitzley, www.bagladyemporium.com: 4r, 8l, 15t, 26 bl, 27b, 25t, 31tr, 36 (all images), 37t, 37cr, 37b, 40tr, 41t, 48t

The Bridgeman Art Library: Private Collection/©ADAGP, Paris and DACS, London 2010/Hair ornament by Lalique and pendant by Philippe Wolfers (1858-1929), Lalique, Rene Jules (1860-1945): 11r

Carlton Books Ltd: Jewellery Courtesy Caroline Cox: 48cr /Jewellery Courtesy Lisa Dyer: 57

Corbis: Blue Lantern Studio: 26t /Christie's Images: 9r /Condé Nast Archive: 8, 16, 22, 28, 31br, 34, 38, 42, 45, 40bl, 46, 50, 53t, 54 /Philippe Eranian: 37cl (panther) / Hulton-Deutsch Collection: 6 /Douglas Kirkland: 49br /Mucha Trust: 10 /Swim Ink: 14tr, /Sygma: 15br

Courtesy of Drucker Antiques: 9t

Enchantiques: Courtesy Erna Kager/www.enchantiques.nl: 37cl (red brooch)

Getty: General Photographic Agency: 18bl /Hulton Archive: 15bl, 40br /John Kobal Foundation: 83c /SSPL: 41b /Time & Life Pictures: 40tl

The Jewelry Stylist: Courtesy of Melinda Lewis, The Jewelry Stylist/Photographic Editor Darrel Chua: 1

Let's Get Vintage: www.letsgetvintage.com: 143b (all flower brooches)

Marjorie K Schick: Photo: Gary Pollmiller: 52 (both images), 53b

Mary Evans Picture Library: 9l /Imagno: 14tl /National Magazine Company: 24br, 41c

Morning Glory Antiques & Jewelry: www.morninggloryjewelry.com: 4cr, 32–3 (all images)

Museum of Arts & Design, New York: Gift of the artists, 2001: 44b

Past Perfect Vintage:/www.pastperfectvintage.com/Courtesy Holly Jenkins-Evans: 4cl, 4c, 18tr, 18cb, 18br, 19c, 19b, 26br, 25b

Penelope's Pearls Vintage & Antique Jewellery: Nancy Bohm: 5c

Picture Desk/Art Archive: Alfredo Dagli Orti: 30cl, 31bl/Museum of London: 8r

Rex Features: Roger-Viollet: 43t

Sipa Press: Unimedia International: 49bl

Topfoto.co.uk: 24t, 48cl /The Granger Collection: 30tr /Land Lost Content/HIP: 48b

Two Silly Magpies Inc.: 2-3, 5cr, 56

Victoria & Albert Museum/V&A Images: 4l, 14b, 20, 21r, 19t /©ADAGP, Paris and DACS, London 2010: 21l /Roger Doyle: 49t /©David Watkins & Wendy Ramshaw: 44t

Every effort has been made to acknowledge correctly and contact the source and/or copyright holder of each picture and Carlton Books Limited apologizes for any unintentional errors or omissions, which will be corrected in future editions of this book.

Further Reading

Art Deco Jewelry, Laurence Mouillefarine and Evelyne Possémé, Thames & Hudson, 2009.

Art Nouveau Jewelry, Vivienne Becker, Thames & Hudson, 1998.

Charmed Bracelet, Tracey Zabar, Stewart, Tabori & Chang, 2004.

A Collector's Guide to Costume Jewelry, Tracy Tolkien and Henrietta Wilkinson, Thames & Hudson, 1997.

Costume Jewellery, Judith Miller, Dorling Kindersley, 2007.

Jewels and Jewellery, Clare Phillips, V & A Publications, 2000.

Rough Diamonds: The Butler & Wilson Collection, Vivienne Becker, Pavilion Books, 1990.

Understanding Jewellery, David Bennett & Daniella Mascetti, Antique Collector's Club, 2010.

Vintage Costume Jewellery: A Passion for Fabulous Fake, Carole Tannenbaum, Antique Colllector's Club, 2005.

Author Acknowledgements

Thanks to the wonderful three "Ms": Marnie, Maggie and Mary, Katy Lubin for her insight into pearls, genius Sheila Ableman, lovely Lionel Marsden, the ever-dapper Khalid Siddiqui, my mates at Sassoon and Lisa Dyer and all at Carlton Books.